Attacked!

Attacked!

By Beasts of Prey and Other Deadly Creatures

◆

True Stories of Survivors

Edited by **John Long**

RAGGED MOUNTAIN PRESS
Camden, Maine

International Marine/
Ragged Mountain Press

A Division of The **McGraw·Hill** *Companies*

10   9   8   7   6   5   4

Printed in the United States of America.

Library of Congress Cataloging-in-Publication Data

Attacked! : by beasts of prey and other deadly creatures : true
    stories of survivors / John Long, editor.
        p.   cm.
    Includes bibliographical references.
    ISBN 0-07-038699-4
    1. Animal attacks—Anecdotes.   2. Predatory animals—Anecdotes.
    I. Long, John, 1954-
    QL100.5.A77   1997
    591.5'3—dc21   97-34529
                                                                        CIP

Questions regarding the content of this book should be addressed to:

Ragged Mountain Press
P.O. Box 220
Camden, ME 04843

Questions regarding the ordering of this book should be addressed to:

The McGraw-Hill Companies
Customer Service Department
P.O. Box 547
Blacklick, OH 43004
Retail customers: 1-800-262-4729
Bookstores: 1-800-233-4726

A portion of the profits from the sale of each Ragged Mountain Press book is donated to an environmental cause.

Printed by R.R. Donnelley
Design and Production by University Graphics, York, PA

Permission information can be found in the credits, p. 205.

Consider the chief of beasts, the crocodile
Who devours cattle as if they were grass.
What strength in his loins.
What power in the muscles of his belly.
His tail is rigid as a cedar,
The sinews of his flanks are closely knit.
His bones are like tubes of bronze.
And his limbs like bars of iron.
He is the chief of God's works,
Made to be a tyrant over his prey.
And in his jaws he crushes all wild beasts.
There under the lotus plant he lies
Hidden in the reeds and the marsh.
The lotus flower conceals him in its shadow . . .

—THE BOOK OF JOB

Contents

Preface

Fear of animal attack has been with us since the dawn of history. In part, human culture and civilization were fashioned to remove the menace of wild animals, to spare us the terror that shot through all who ever battled a big predator on its own terms. A safe place to hang our hats is a welcome thing; but it can never silence the bear's roar, echoing through our unconscious memories. If you doubt it, go to the zoo and stare into the eyes of the mighty grizzly and listen to its growl, which comes from the middle of the earth. Here, we are face to face with what it all comes down to in the end, the irreducible brute element. And here, according to Sy Montgomery, "is when you know, for the first time, that your body is made of meat."

For those of us in the developed countries, getting mauled by a grizzly bear, say, is a notion as remote as Mars. But if we read on, and allow ourselves to be carried away in the vortex of these narratives, we find ourselves facing the beast itself. And we feel it in our guts. These stories make time travelers of us all, casting us back to an age when the big predators reigned. These are not our personal stories, but they are true chapters in our collective histories, a chronicle richer and wilder than we might ever imagine—until we start turning these pages.

Several of the following stories are from professional hunters; others come from those who were merely passing through a predator's domain for recreation or science. Brief afterwords explore possible reasons for the attacks, and look a little into the minds and hearts of those who hunted man-eaters, were attacked by them, or both. On the surface, these accounts are page turners. Yet, when we look past the flashing teeth and consider the victim's thoughts, feelings, and reactions as a savage predator tore into them, we sometimes discover the miraculous. Hanging is said to have had a wonderful capacity to "condense the mind." So it is with attack by wild animals. Crisis and trauma have always been a call to action through which people come to answer, in one form or another, the fundamental questions: Who are we? What truly matters? What do we do? I trust these stories throw some unexpected light on these questions.

A fascinating subtext to these accounts concerns legends like Captain Jim Corbett, Peter Hathaway Capstick, and Pat James Byrne, professionals who pitted their lives against rogue elephants and man-eating tigers. When weighing the honest-to-God motives of such men, we're often left with specious terms like pluck, machismo, and duty. However, when these people tell their own stories—as they've done so wonderfully in this volume—they quickly debunk the myth of fearlessness and intimate motives that, even if perfectly true, are so slippery they have no name in any language. Ultimately it all harks back to the age-old question of why the man climbed the terrible mountain. It is an invitation to wrestle one of the Great Mysteries: that only to the extent that we expose ourselves over and over again to annihilation can the indestructible arise within us. In this, according to philosopher Karlfried Graf, lies the "dignity of daring," and the "reason" why a person would track a wounded leopard into dark and tangled bush.

With every passing year, the wilderness seems to shrink a little, and the big predators have that much less room to roam, to be what nature made them. In such places we will always be intruders, and mere trespass through a predator's domain may occasionally be enough to incite an aggressive response. Tragically, many have become obsessed with making our wilderness areas "safe." Rather than trying to make our schools or cities safe, our misguided frustrations are taken out on animals, and the little ground they can still call their own. Some people will crush anything that poses a threat to their control and dominion; but they miss the majestic thought that we are all voyagers through a realm of natural forces that far outshine our own. Peter Capstick said it perfectly:

> The KiSwahili speakers understand the lion's long roar best, I think, interpreting the hollow, echoing challenge of Simba that rolls across the liquid darkness of rivers and the muted dun of plain from incredible miles as follows:
>
> "Hi inchi ya nani?" translate the tribesmen with the suppression of a shudder. "Whose land is this?"
>
> "Yangu, yangu, yangu."
>
> "Mine, mine, mine."

Lion Attack!

Peter Hathaway Capstick

Authorities have likened man-eating lions to homicidal maniacs among men; indeed, there are apparently some lions that kill just for the hell of it, but the most common cause of man-eating in Africa is the most obvious: hunger. If a lion is hungry enough, he will eat you. Period. Consider the case in Wankie National Park, Rhodesia, of the lions that in 1972 gave two families a night of indescribable horror. Here is the story as I obtained it from direct interview at the time.

Len Harvey, a Rhodesian game warden, had recently been married and was honeymoon camping with his wife, Jean, at an old elephant control station near the Shapi *pan,* as natural ponds and flowages are called. At Shapi was another semivacationing ranger and his family, an experienced man named Willy De Beer, his wife, daughter, and her husband, a student from Salisbury called Colin Matthews. In a two-day period, three lions had become increasingly bold, even to the point of entering the camp and eating chickens belonging to the native staff. However, since they had attacked no one and were within the borders of the national park, nothing could be done despite their threatening behavior.

The second night, firearms locked away in accordance with regulations designed to prevent their theft for guerrilla purposes, Len and Jean were asleep in a pole-and-dagga (mud) hut. Slightly after 11 P.M. a large lioness leaped through the window of the hut, hurling Jean from her bed to the floor. Instantly the lioness bit her through the small of the back and shook her like a terrier with a lamb chop. Shrieking with pain and terror, the woman struggled to escape. Shocked awake, Len Harvey realized what was happening and, with the incredible bravery of the desperate, threw himself on the lioness barehanded, punching and scratching to make the big cat drop his wife. It did. In one lightning movement it flattened the man, driving long fangs deep into his shoulder. Still conscious, Len screamed for his wife to get out of the hut and run. She rolled under the bed and, hysterical with agony and fear, emerged from the far side of the hut near the door. Covered with gore from her wounds, she fled the black hut but, halfway to the De Beer house, she stopped, giving a desperate thought to helping her husband. As she neared the hut again with steel nerve, there was a scuffle of movement, and although she was a young woman who had never listened to anyone die, the sound that came through the darkness left no doubt that Len Harvey was beyond help.

Banging on the De Beers' door, she poured out her story and collapsed. Willy awoke his son-in-law and sent him to start the small Honda generator while he went to the storeroom for the guns. In the light of the small room he grabbed a Model 70 Winchester in .375 H&H caliber, and a Parker-Hale .243, both bolt-action rifles, along with a handful of cartridges for each. Fumbling, he loaded them both, jacking a round into each chamber. Locking the safety catches, he handed the .243 to Colin Matthews as he came up. Both men, still in their underwear, ran for the Harvey hut. The door was shut.

De Beer looked the hut over carefully. Seeing and hearing nothing, he called Harvey's name softly. A deep, warning snarl cut the thin light of the naked bulb outside the hut and De Beer cursed. Still inside. He edged up to the window, a small, black orifice in the mud wall. The safety snicked off the .375 as the Rhodesian paused. What if Len wasn't dead but only unconscious? A blind shot might kill him. He would have to be able to see the lioness to risk a safe shot. Gritting his teeth, he eased his head into the window, catching a glimpse of Harvey's bloody legs in a thin bar of light. But he did not see the paw stroke that tore through the skin of his forehead and grated on his skull bone. A sheet of blood burst into his eyes as he threw himself backward, gasping in pain.

Most men who had just had their foreheads ripped open by a man-eating lioness would not be anxious for an encore performance. Willy De Beer was not most men. Directing Colin Matthews to rip his T-shirt into strips, he had the young man bind the wound to keep the blood out of his eyes. Shortening up on the rifle, he approached the window once more. Waves of agony made him gag and wobble, but he pushed the rifle barrel through the window again. This time the lioness was ready and waiting for him. She lashed out of the blackness and caught De Beer behind the head at the base of the skull, the two-inch talons driving to bone and holding him like great fishhooks. The cat tried to drag him into the hut with her, but De Beer screamed, let the rifle fall through the window into the hut, and, gripping the edges of the opening with both hands, tried to push away. The lioness' breath gagged him as she tried to get his face into her mouth, but, because the paw she was holding him with was in the way, she failed. The man-eater gave a terrific tug and the claws ripped forward, tearing De Beer's scalp loose from his skull until it hung over his face like a dripping, hairy, red beret. The man fell backward onto the ground, and the lioness immediately launched herself through the window after him, landing on his prostrate body.

Although barely conscious, Willy De Beer had the presence of mind to try to cover his mutilated head with his hands, a feat he accomplished just as the man-eater grabbed his head in her jaws and started to drag him away. Perhaps covering his head was a conscious gesture, perhaps reflex. Whichever, it probably saved his life. As the lioness lay chewing on his head, she may have thought that the crushing sounds she heard beneath her teeth were the breaking of the skull bone instead of those of the man's hands and fingers. De Beer, completely blind and helpless, could only scream as the lioness ate him alive.

Ten feet away, petrified with terror, Colin Matthews stood watching the cat ravage his father-in-law. In his white-knuckled fists was the .243 rifle, loaded with four 100-grain soft-point slugs and a fifth in the chamber. Colin could have easily shot the man-eater, but he did not. Never having fired a rifle before, he did not know where the safety catch was or even that there was one. As he fought with the little Parker-Hale to make it fire, the incredible, unbelievable, unthinkable happened: Colin Matthews put his foot into a galvanized bucket hidden in the shadows, lost his balance, and fell, dropping the precious rifle.

The lioness looked up, her bloody mouth twisted into a snarl. She had been too busy with Willy De Beer to realize Matthews' presence but suddenly dropped the ranger and, with a hair-raising roar, charged the prostrate boy. Matthews was still struggling to remove the bucket from his foot when the lioness slammed into him. As if in a dream, he shoved his right arm as far as it would go into the enraged animal's mouth, the wood-rasp tongue tight in his fist. White flares of agony rocketed up his arm as the powerful teeth met against his bones, crushing them like pretzel sticks.

Slowly the blind, semiconscious De Beer realized that the great weight was gone, that the lioness wasn't biting him anymore. As from a long distance, he could hear Colin shrieking over his pain. He rolled over, face-up on the dirt, listening to the lion chewing on the young man. Automatically his crushed hands began to feel around for a weapon, anything. His broken fingers touched something hard: in a flash he realized that it was a rifle barrel, the fallen .243. Ignoring the agony of broken bones, he tried to grasp it. It seemed stuck. It dawned on him that the lioness must be standing on the stock. Somehow he tugged it free, the sudden release making him fall backward. Awkwardly, he reversed the rifle, found the safety, and, still unseeing, listened to determine where to fire. By the sounds, the lioness was standing over Colin's body. He triggered the first shot, then, as fast as his smashed hands could work the bolt action, fired twice more. Silence blanketed the camp.

"Colin! Are you all right? Colin!"

"Yes, Dad, I'm all right," answered a pain-tight voice. "But you've shot my hand off."

"Before De Beer could answer, Matthews gave another scream, which mixed with a grunt from the dying lioness. In her death throes, she had moved down the young man's body and, in a final reflex, bitten the kneecap completely off Colin's leg. On De Beer's legs and Matthew's eyes, they staggered back to the house where Mrs. De Beer drove the thirty miles to Main Camp, Wankie, for the Rhodesian army helicopter that evacuated the victims at five the next morning.

Rescuers found Len Harvey's body where it lay in the hut, partially eaten by the lioness. He was buried the next day. A post-mortem on the lioness revealed no reason for her attack beyond hunger. Her stomach contained a small snake, a wad of chicken feathers, and most of Len Harvey's face. The first shot fired by De Beer had caught her in the lungs, the second in the shoulder, and the third, traveling at a muzzle velocity of 3,000 feet per second, pierced the cat's right cheek, completely smashed Colin's hand and knuckles, which were inside the lioness' mouth, and then passed harmlessly through the left cheek. An inch or so higher or lower would have broken either her upper or lower jaw and prevented her from snapping off Colin's kneecap a few seconds later. The luck of the draw.

Willy De Beer, surprisingly, survived his wounds. He had 222 stitches in his head alone and immense skin and bone grafting work on both head and hands. Two months after the attack his head was still swollen twice the normal size, and he continued to suffer from dizziness and ringing in the ears. Colin Matthews had had many operations on his hand, but it is not expected to be of much use to him again. His knee may someday support his weight once more, but that won't be determined until years of grafting operations have been completed. Widow Jean Harvey recovered from her bites, if not her nightmares, and was released from the hospital within two months of the tragic night.

---◆---

In the years after the events in this story took place, Rhodesia shook off decades of colonial rule and became the independent nation of Zimbabwe. Expatriate English, Dutch, and white South Africans (like the principals in this story) no longer run the game reserves or lock their guns away from guerrillas. But like guerrillas, the big predators have remained much the same: aggressive, territorial, and lethal when crossed.

Chesterson said that courage is a paradox, that a man must be a little careless of his life so as to keep it. But did Len Harvey think there was any chance of keeping his own life when he yelled for his wife to flee as a starving lion tore into him? And what of Willie De Beer, who suffered a terrible mauling while trying to save the doomed Len Harvey? Our tongues say that Len Harvey and Willie De Beer did the right and noble thing, but would our bodies obey our words if we were there? And what of a cat so swift and agile that it could strike a man twice before he could get off a shot from a ready rifle? And who can fathom De Beers's situation as he wrestled the 500-pound lion while his jinxed son-in-law fumbled with the safety on his rifle before stepping into a bucket? Although these things are almost beyond imagining, if we push past the grisly and unlucky details and reflect on these people's deeds we can appreciate that—even in the face of an attack by savage animals—courage is a basic endowment imperishable as love and kindness. This theme is richly played out in attack stories, and its depth is even more evident in the animal kingdom, for rare is the mother beast who will not give her own life to defend her young.

As far as lions go, experts insist that such bold, brutal attacks are freak occurrences spurred by starvation that leads to such extreme behavior as a means of survival and that becomes the immediate challenge to everyone in the predator's orbit.

J.L.

———◆———

Rage on the River Zambezi

John Dyson

"**W**elcome to the mighty Zambezi!," Paul Templer said to the six tourists he was about to lead on a three-hour trip down one of Africa's longest rivers. Heading onward toward thundering Victoria Falls in Zimbabwe, the group hoped to see elephants, crocodiles and hippopotamuses along the way. It was a perfect afternoon in March 1996, with a cool sky and mild breeze.

The 27-year-old guide briefed the three couples. "We call it the 'royal drift' because we do the paddling and your job is to sit back and relax," Templer said. Then he motioned toward the revolver in a holster at his belt. "But there are dangers," he warned. "The river's full of crocodiles, so don't trail your hand in the water. It will look like a fish, and that's what crocs snack on. The next hazard is hippos," Templer continued. "Hippos are territorial, so we know which areas to avoid. But a hippo having a bad day might decide to bump your canoe."

Templler grinned as his clients gasped. "A big hip could tip you into the water. If that happens, don't panic. It won't eat you. Hippos are vegetarians." Templer's team included freelance canoeing guide Mike McNamara, 31, who was accompanying the team in a kayak, and canoe paddlers Ben Sibands, 24, and Evans Namasango, a cheerful, hard-working 22-year-old who had recently taken the exams to qualify as an apprentice guide. Templer had liked Namasango from the start and tutored him almost daily.

Templer divided the tourists. In his boat were Guaiacum Stahmann and his wife, Gundi, from the outskirts of Bremen, Germany. In Sibanda's canoe were Murielle Fischer and her fiancé, Pierre Lagardère, while Nathalie Grassot and Marc Skorupka went with Namasango; the four tourists were all Air France employees.

Templer's heart was singing as the little flotilla pushed out into the Zambezi's gentle current. He had grown up with one foot in the bush, living mainly on remote military bases. His father had been an officer for the former British colony of South Rhodesia before it became Zimbabwe. With the barnyard shoulders of a butterfly swimmer and the rugged torso of a rugby star, Templer was a gifted athlete with a streak of recklessness. While working in Israel, he'd tried to drive a tractor across a minefield into Jordan to buy beer. The prank got him booted from the country.

Back home in Zimbabwe, he was camping with friends on the shore of Lake Kariba when a canoe safari drifted by. *That's the way to go!* he told himself. With his usual gung-ho enthusiasm, he knocked off what was normally a year-long course in law, ballistics and natural history in three months to pass the stiff exams required to become a professional river guide. Templer was made for the job, and for more than 18 months he had overseen canoe trips for Frontiers Tours.

As a professional guide, Templer's job was to bring tourists and wildlife together; but not too close together. Once he intercepted several Japanese visitors as they were walking casually toward several mature, male lions, cameras clicking.

And there were hippos, one of Africa's most dangerous animals. In a bull hippo, the two central lower teeth, up to eight inches long, poke straight from it's cavernous mouth like the bars of a forklift. The two massive canine teeth curving down from the top of the jaw slide against the two jutting up from below, keeping them sharp as the blades of hedge cutters.

Every so often hippos bumped a canoe, sometime spilling passengers into the river. One guide had lost a leg to a hippo two years before. And only six months ago, a big bull hippo suddenly smacked the bottom of Templer's canoe, catapulting him and two passengers into the water. The same hippo chased and bumped other canoes as well. Soon the close-knit river guides were passing word about the rogue's locale so it could be avoided. But now, as Templer led the flotilla through a gauntlet of rocky islands, he did not know that the rogue hippo had moved. He was leading the flotilla straight to the animal's new territory.

Templer's canoe drifted lazily just a paddle's length from the shoreline of an island. Barely thirty yards away was a herd of hippos, their dark hides red with a secretion that protects them from sunburn, giving rise to the idea that they sweat blood. In a whisper Templer explained that hippos could be five feet high at the shoulders, fourteen feet from snout to tail-tip and weigh several tons. "That's more than my BMW," Guaiacum Stahmann thought.

"Let's move on," Templer said, dipping his paddle. As they passed a mother hippo lying in the water, her calf dozing with its chin on her back, the sun was dropping toward the treetops. In forty minutes, Templer knew, the group must be at the landing where a truck would take the tourists back to their hotels.

McNamara bumped his kayak down a wide, foot-high ledge of rock over which the river cascaded into a pool about two-hundred feet across. Sibanda, angling into the current, was next, with Templer and then Namasango following close behind. Templer rapped his canoe to encourage any hippos hidden below to surface, so the paddlers could avoid them. Suddenly there was a noise like a thunderclap. Bam! A bull hippo hit Namasango's canoe, throwing the back three feet into the air and hurling Namasango out.

Templer whipped around in his seat to see the back end of Namasango's canoe on the shoulders of a hippo—the rogue hippo. The great beast opened its huge mouth, then submerged abruptly. As the canoe's two remaining passengers, Grossot and Skorupa, fought to keep it level, Namasango bobbed up in the water, gasping.

Templer back-paddled his canoe toward Namasango. "Hold on, I'm on my way!" he yelled.

Left without a paddler or spare paddle, Grassot and Skorupka worked the water madly with their hands to get out of the hippos reach. Sibanda, who was now bringing up the rear, turned his canoe into the shallows a few yards away; his passengers Fischer and Lagardere scrambled onto a rocky outcrop.

Namasango reached for the side of Templer's canoe. Templer saw the risk of being capsized at that angle. "No. Come around back," he told Namasango. With one stroke Templer positioned the back of his canoe within Namasango's reach. "The hippo won't return," he told himself. The Stahmanns leaned to the right, balancing the canoe as Templer twisted left and leaned out of the boat, extending a hand for Namasango to grab.

Their fingers were just inches apart when the hippo exploded out of the water like a pickup truck with its hood open. Water and spray flew from its muzzle; a roar like a gunned engine blasted from its pink-and-orange throat. In an instant the hippo took Templer into its mouth headfirst. It's huge upper teeth pierced his armpits, then punctured the small of his back, pinning both arms to his sides. Then the beast disappeared beneath the surface again. So cleanly did it happen that Templer's canoe remained upright for one long moment before it slowly toppled, dumping the Stahmanns into the river.

Pulling Templer twelve feet underwater, the hippo played with the two-hundred-pound man like a dog with a rag doll. Templer, face-down in the Hippo's mouth, didn't know where he was. Everything was black. "Am I inside something?" he wondered. Suddenly the viselike pressure came off Templer's chest. As the Hippo opened his jaws, Templer got one arm free and felt and felt around wildly. His fingers felt the coarse bristles of the hippo's snout.

Jackknifing his body to get leverage, Templer pushed with all his might. He felt strangely calm, as if watching himself in a film. His other arm came free and he found a leathery lip to push on. The hippo's teeth gnashed his cheeks and the back of his head. Suddenly it released him and Templer swam toward the light.

His head shot out of the water, blood gushing down his face. The first thing he saw was Namasango, gasping and struggling to tread water.

"Swim, Evans! We're going to the side!" Templer yelled. But Namasango seemed to be in shock. So Templer took his chin in the crook of his bloody elbow and pulled him toward the riverbank.

Suddenly Templer felt his leg pinned by an enormous weight—the hippo was back! This time it grabbed Templer from below, its mammoth tooth boring through his foot, pulling him under. Templer released his grip on Namasango, hoping that he would reach the surface.

Templer knew that a hippo could stay underwater for six-minutes—and knew that in his injured state, he could last only one, possibly two before he'd drown. In a frenzy of desperation, Templer kicked and clawed at the hippos snout. His pinioned leg came free but now his arm was jammed in the beast's mouth. Templer summoned his ebbing strength for more blows on the bristly snout. Let go of me! And suddenly, it did.

When McNamara saw Templer's head break the surface, he swung his kayak toward him and yelled, "Swim to me!"

But the hippo got there first. Thrusting its body half out of the water, the beast snatched Templer's torso in his jaws. Templer's head and shoulders hung out of one side of the hippo's mouth, his legs out the other. His left arm was slashed between a pair of scissoring canines and two teeth bored into his chest. Templer felt his ribs being splintered.

In a rage, the hippo started dunking Templer in and out of the water. A geyser of bright red blood spurted from Templer's side as the hippo's teeth cut an artery.

Templer felt his body being whipped left and right, up and down. With his free hand he tried to reach his revolver but discovered that it was gone. He was out of breath, and his mind was beginning to blur. "I can't take anymore," he thought. But he continued to fight, punching the hippo's tough hide with his free hand.

Suddenly, the hippo spat Templer into the water and left him. He bobbed up next to McNamara's kayak. "Get me out of here," he mumbled, grabbing the kayak's rope.

As McNamara pulled him to shallow water, Templer's first thought was to rescue the people he was responsible for. "We have to get them to the bank," he said, gasping. "Where's Evans?"

Fischer and Lagardere saw Evans Namasango appear on the surface about fifty yards downriver. He waved his arm above the water, then sank. The hippo, leaping like a horse, burst clear out of the water and landed on the spot where Namasango had just been.

Then the pain hit Templer, and he slumped in the water. "It chewed me up pretty badly," he said, groaning.

Inside Templer's tattered left sleeve, McNamara saw a mess.

The upper arm was crushed in two places, the lower part stripped of flesh. He had lost a lot of blood from the wounds in the sides of his chest, and his left foot was crushed to a pulp. One lung was visible through a gaping hole in his back.

The first-aid box and two-way radio were lost when Templer's canoe was overturned. When they got him to the sandbank, Templer complained that he could feel his lungs filling with blood. McNamara ripped the cellophane wrap off their snack food and sealed the holes in Templer's chest, hoping to prevent his lungs from collapsing.

Sibanda snatched up his paddle. "Go!" McNamara told him, pushing the canoe out into the current. "Paul's going downhill fast," McNamara thought. "He won't make it."

In six minutes of all out paddling, Sibanda reached the landing. By chance the local medical rescue team was conducting an emergency drill. They drove Templer to the local hospital, but it had no surgeon. The nearest one was 270 miles away in Bulawayo.

When Templer arrived there at one a.m., orthopedist Bekithemba Ncube, 41, was waiting. The patient was a mess, but he could have been worse. Had the axillary artery in one armpit not been cut so cleanly that it sealed itself, Templer would have bled to death in less than one minute. Had the massive puncture wounds in his back not been made at an angle, which created flaps that stopped air leaking into his chest, his lungs would have totally collapsed. In a seven-hour operation, Ncube patched him up and amputated the mangled left arm.

After two days of searching, Evans Namasango's remains were found downriver. Undaunted, the river guide, now fitted with a prosthetic arm, has returned to the bush to run expeditions in Zimbabwe, Namibia, and Botswana.

Although professional hunters urged the Zimbabwe Department of National Parks and Wildlife to shoot the rogue hippo, it is still in the river. Waiting . . .

◆

After this story first appeared, some readers were surprised by the ferocity of the attack and even that the attack happened at all. Yet we all know aggression is an impulse running through everything alive. Many peaceable herbivores, both big and small, will occasionally attack without apparent regard for their own lives. Cross such animals at the wrong time or in the wrong place and brace yourself for an assault of some kind.

Notice in this story, and in others in this collection, how the victim's mind became clear and detached even in the midst of a near-fatal attack. No less intriguing is the victim's concern for the safety of others in his party. Here, Paul Templer, even after a ghastly mauling, kept trying to do his job as a river guide until he was completely disabled.

Why do victims' minds become lucid and detached during attack? What of their common concern for the safety of others even while a wild beast rips them apart? These are questions for the ages, but they show us that if we look beneath the wounds, we find there is more going on than meets the eye. At our core, part of us is not as frightened nor as petty as we sometimes feel.

Official statistics regarding the frequency of hippo attacks are lacking, but it's well established that few animals are more territorial than bull hippos. According to African river guides who frequent hippo habitat, although outright attack is rare, harassment—usually in the form of ramming or even biting through neoprene rafts—is not uncommon. Commercial guides understand the inherent risk of rubbing elbows with beasts that routinely weigh more than a ton and are willing to take those risks. Or they were. I wonder if African river guides who have heard Templer's story ply the water thinking about him thrashing in the rogue's mouth, his legs sticking out one side and his head, the other.

Most experts agree that the only sure way to avoid a hippo attack is to give the animal the widest possible berth. Because hippos rarely stray far from water and usually cluster together, a wilderness traveler can know where hippos will be and can take measures to avoid them.

J.L.

The Muktesar Man-Eater

Jim Corbett

Eighteen miles to the north-northeast of Naini Tal is a hill eight thousand feet high and twelve to fifteen miles long, running east and west. The western end of the hill rises steeply and near this end is the Muktesar Veterinary Research Institute, where lymph and vaccines are produced to fight India's cattle diseases. The laboratory and staff quarters are situated on the northern face of the hill and command one of the best views to be had anywhere of the Himalayan snowy range. This range, and all the hills that lie between it and the plains of India, run east and west, and from a commanding point on any of the hills an uninterrupted view can be obtained not only of the snows to the north but also of the hills and valleys to the east and to the west as far as the eye can see. People who have lived at Muktesar claim that it is the most beautiful spot in Kumaon, and that its climate has no equal.

A tigress that thought as highly of the amenities of Muktesar as human beings did, took up her residence in the extensive forests adjoining the small settlement. Here she lived very happily on *sambhar, kakar* and wild pig, until she had the misfortune to have an encounter with a porcupine. In this encounter she lost an eye and got some fifty quills, varying in length from one to nine inches, embedded in the arm and under the pad of her right foreleg. Several of these quills after striking a bone had doubled back in the form of a U, the point and the broken-off end being close together. Suppurating sores formed where she endeavored to extract the quills with her teeth, and while she was lying up in a thick patch of grass, starving and licking her wounds, a woman selected this particular patch of grass to cut as fodder for her cattle. At first the tigress took no notice, but when the woman had cut the grass right up to where she was lying, the tigress struck once, the blow crushing in the woman's skull. Death was instantaneous, for, when found the following day, she was grasping her sickle with one hand and holding a tuft of grass, which she was about to cut when struck, with the other. Leaving the woman lying where she had fallen, the tigress limped off for a distance of over a mile and took refuge in a little hollow under a fallen tree. Two days later a man came to chip firewood off this fallen tree, and the tigress who was lying on the far side killed him also. The man fell across the tree, and as he had removed his coat and shirt and the tigress had clawed his back when killing him, it is possible that the sight of blood trickling down his body as he hung across the bole of the tree first gave her the idea that he was something that she could satisfy her hunger with. However that may be, before leaving him she ate a small portion from his back. A day later she killed her third victim deliberately, and without having received any provocation. Thereafter she became an established man-eater.

I heard of the tigress shortly after she started killing human beings, and as there were a number of sportsmen at Muktesar, all of whom were keen on bagging the tigress—who was operating right on their doorsteps—I did not consider it would be sporting of an outsider to meddle in the matter. When the toll of human beings killed by the tigress had risen to twenty-four, however, and the lives of all the people living in the settlement and neighboring villages were endangered and work at the Institute slowed down, the veterinary officer in charge of the Institute requested Government to solicit my help.

My task, as I saw it, was not going to be an easy one, for, apart from the fact that my experience of man-eaters was very limited, the extensive ground over which the tigress was operating was not known to me and I therefore had no idea where to look for her.

Accompanied by a servant and two men carrying a roll of bedding and a suitcase, I left Naini Tal at midday and walked ten miles to the Ramgarh dak bungalow, where I spent the night. The dak bungalow *khansama* (cook, bottle-washer, and general factotum) was a friend of mine, and when he learnt that I was on my way to Muktesar to try to shoot the man-eater, he warned me to be very careful while negotiating the last two miles into Muktesar for, he said, several people had recently been killed on that stretch of the road.

Leaving my men to pack up and follow me I armed myself with a double-barrelled .500 express rifle using modified cordite, and making a very early start the next morning I arrived at the junction of the Naini Tal/Almora road with the Muktesar road just as it was getting light. From this point it was necessary to walk warily for I was now in the man-eater's country. Before zigzagging up the face of a very steep hill the road runs for some distance over flat ground on which grows the orange-coloured lily, the round hard seeds of which can be used as shot in a muzzle-loading gun. This was the first time I had ever climbed that hill and I was very interested to see the caves, hollowed out by wind, in the sandstone cliffs overhanging the road. In a gale I imagine these caves must produce some very weird sounds, for they are of different sizes and, while some are shallow, others appear to penetrate deep into the sandstone.

Where the road comes out on a saddle of the hill there is a small area of flat ground flanked on the far side by the Muktesar Post Office, and a small bazaar. The post office was not open at that early hour, but one of the shops was and the shopkeeper very kindly gave me directions how to find the dak bungalow, which he said was half a mile away on the northern face of the hill. There are two dak bungalows at Muktesar, one reserved for government officials and the other for the general public. I did not know this and my shop-keeper friend, mistaking me for a government official, possibly because of the size of my hat, directed me to the wrong one and the *khansama* in charge of the bungalow, and I, incurred the displeasure of the red tape brigade, the *khansama* by providing me with breakfast, and I by partaking of it. However, of this I was at the time happily ignorant, and later I made it my business to see that the *khansama* did not suffer in any way for my mistake.

While I was admiring the superb view of the snowy range, and waiting for breakfast, a party of twelve Europeans passed me carrying service rifles, followed a few minutes later by a sergeant and two men carrying targets and flags. The sergeant, a friendly soul, informed me that the party that had just passed was on its way to the rifle range, and that it was keeping together because of the man-eater. I learnt from the sergeant that the officer in charge of the Institute had received a telegram from Government the previous day informing him that I was on my way to Muktesar. The sergeant expressed the hope that I would succeed in shooting the man-eater for, he said, conditions in the settlement had become very difficult. No one, even in daylight, cared to move about alone, and after dusk everyone had to remain behind locked doors. Many attempts had been made to shoot the man-eater but it had never returned to any of the kills that had been sat over.

After a very good breakfast I instructed the *khansama* to tell my men when they arrived that I had gone out to try to get news of the man-eater, and that I did not know when I would return. Then, picking up my rifle, I went up to the post office to send a telegram to my mother to let her know I had arrived safely.

From the flat ground in front of the post office and the bazaar the southern face of the Muktesar hill falls steeply away, and is cut up by ridges and ravines overgrown with dense brushwood, with a few trees scattered here and there. I was standing on the edge of the hill, looking down into the valley and the well-wooded Ramgarh hills beyond, when I was joined by the Postmaster and several shopkeepers. The Postmaster had dealt with the Government telegram of the previous day, and on seeing my signature on the form I had just handed in, he concluded I was the person referred to in the telegram and he and his friends had now come to offer me their help. I was very glad of the offer for they were in the best position to see and converse with everyone coming to Muktesar, and as the man-eater was sure to be the main topic of conversation where two or more were gathered together, they would be able to collect information that would be of great value to me. In rural India the post office and the *bania's* shop are to village folk what taverns and clubs are to people of other lands, and if information on any particular subject is sought, the post office and the *bania's* shop are the best places to seek it.

In a fold of the hill to our left front, and about two miles away and a thousand feet below us, was a patch of cultivation. This I was informed was Badri Sah's apple orchard. Badri, son of an old friend of mine, had visited me in Naini Tal some months previously and had offered to put me up in this guest house and to assist me in every way he could to shoot the man-eater. This offer, for the reason already given, I had not accepted. Now, however, as I had come to Muktesar at the request of the Government I decided I would call on

Badri and accept his offer to help me, especially as I had just been informed by my companions that the last human kill had taken place in the valley below his orchard.

Thanking all the men who were standing round me, and telling them I would rely on them for further information, I set off down the Dhari road. The day was still young and before calling on Badri there was time to visit some of the villages farther along the hill to the east. There were no milestones along the road, and after I had covered what I considered was about six miles and visited two villages I turned back. I had retraced my steps for about three miles when I overtook a small girl in difficulties with a bullock. The girl, who was about eight years old, wanted the bullock to go in the direction of Muktesar, while the bullock wanted to go in the opposite direction, and when I arrived on the scene the stage had been reached when neither would do what the other wanted. The bullock was a quiet old beast, and with the girl walking in front holding the rope that was tied round his neck and I walking behind to keep him on the move he gave no further trouble. After we had proceeded a short distance I said:

"We are not stealing Kalwa, are we?" I had heard her addressing the black bullock by that name.

"N—o," she answered indignantly, turning her big brown eyes full on me.

"To whom does he belong?" I next asked.

"To my father," she said.

"And where are we taking him?"

"To my uncle."

"And why does uncle want Kalwa?"

"To plough his field."

"But Kalwa can't plough uncle's field by himself."

"Of course not," she said. I *was* being stupid, but then you could not expect a Sahib to know anything about bullocks and ploughing.

"Has uncle only got one bullock?" I next asked.

"Yes," she said; "he has only got one bullock now, but he did have two."

"Where is the other one?" I asked, thinking that it had probably been sold to satisfy a debt.

"The tiger killed it yesterday," I was told. Here was news indeed, and while I was digesting it we walked on in silence, the girl every now and then looking back at me until she plucked up courage to ask:

"Have you come to shoot the tiger?"

"Yes," I said, "I have come to try to shoot the tiger."

"Then why are you going away from the kill?"

"Because we are taking Kalwa to uncle." My answer appeared to satisfy the girl, and we plodded on. I had got some very useful information, but I wanted more and presently I said:

"Don't you know that the tiger is a man-eater?"

"Oh, yes," she said, "it ate Kunthi's father and Bonshi Singh's mother, and lots of other people."

"Then why did your father send you with Kalwa? Why did he not come himself?"

"Because he has *bhabari bokhar* [malaria]."

"Have you no brothers?"

"No. I had a brother but he died long ago."

"A mother?"

"Yes, I have a mother; she is cooking the food."

"A sister?"

"No, I have no sister." So on this small girl had devolved the dangerous task of taking her father's bullock to her uncle, along a road on which men were afraid to walk except when in large parties, and on which in four hours I had not seen another human being.

We had now come to a path up which the girl went, the bullock following, and I bringing up the rear. Presently we came to a field on the far side of which was a small house. As we approached the house the girl called out and told her uncle that she had brought Kalwa.

"All right," a man's voice answered from the house, "tie him to the post, Putli, and go home. I am having my food." So we tied Kalwa to the post and went back to the road. Without the connecting link of Kalwa between us, Putli [dolly] was now shy, and as she would not walk by my side I walked ahead, suiting my pace to hers. We walked in silence for some time, and then I said:

"I want to shoot the tiger that killed uncle's bullock but I don't know where the kill is. Will you show me?"

"Oh, yes," she said eagerly, "I will show you."

"Have you seen the kill?" I asked.

"No," she said, "I have not seen it, but I heard uncle telling my father where it was."

"Is it close to the road?"

"I don't know."

"Was the bullock alone when it was killed?"

"No, it was with the village cattle."

"Was it killed in the morning or the evening?"

"It was killed in the morning when it was going out to graze with the cows."

While talking to the girl I was keeping a sharp look-out all round, for the road was narrow and bordered on the left by heavy tree jungle, and on the right by dense scrub. We had proceeded for about a mile when we came to a well-used cattle track leading off into the jungle on the left. Here the girl stopped and said it was on this track that her uncle had told her father the bullock had been killed. I had now got all the particulars I needed to enable me to find the kill, and after seeing the girl safely to her home I returned to the cattle track. This track ran across a valley and I had gone along it for about a quarter of a mile when I came on a spot where cattle had stampeded. Leaving the track, I now went through the jungle, parallel to and about fifty yards below the track. I had only gone a short distance when I came on a drag-mark. This drag-mark went straight down into the valley and after I had followed it for a few hundred yards I found the bullock, from which only a small portion of the hindquarters had been eaten. It was lying at the foot of a bank about twenty feet high, and some forty feet from the head of a deep ravine. Between the ravine and the kill was a stunted tree, smothered over by a wild rose. This was the only tree within a reasonable distance of the kill on which I could sit with any hope of bagging the tiger, for there was no moon, and if the tiger came after dark—as I felt sure it would—the nearer I was to the kill the better would be my chance of killing the tiger.

It was now 2 P.M. and there was just time for me to call on Badri and ask him for a cup of tea, of which I was in need for I had done a lot of walking since leaving Ramgarh at four o'clock that morning. The road to Badri's orchard takes off close to where the cattle track joins the road, and runs down a steep hill for a mile through dense brushwood. Badri was near his guest house, attending to a damaged apple tree when I arrived, and on hearing the reason for my visit he took me up to the guest house which was on a little knoll overlooking the orchard. While we sat on the veranda waiting for the tea and something to eat that Badri had ordered his servant to prepare for me, I told him why I had come to Muktesar, and about the kill the young girl had enabled me to find. When I asked Badri why this kill had not been reported to the sportsmen at Muktesar, he said that owing to the repeated failures of the sportsmen to bag the tiger the village folk had lost confidence in them, and for this reason kills were no longer being reported to them. Badri attributed the failures to the elaborate preparations that had been made to sit over kills. These preparations consisted of clearing the ground near the kills of all obstructions in the way of bushes and small trees, the building of big *machans,* and the occupation of the *machans* by several men. Reasons enough for the reputation the tiger had earned of never returning to a kill. Badri was convinced that there was only one tiger in the Muktesar district and that it was slightly lame in its right foreleg, but he did not know what had caused the lameness, nor did he know whether the animal was male or female.

Sitting on the veranda with us was a big Airedale terrier. Presently the dog started growling, and looking in the direction in which the dog was facing, we saw a big *langur* sitting on the ground and holding down the branch of an apple tree, and eating the unripe fruit. Picking up a shotgun that was leaning against the railing of the veranda, Badri loaded it with No. 4 shot and fired. The range was too great for the pellets, assuming any hit it, to do the *langur* any harm, but the shot had the effect of making it canter up the hill with the dog in hot pursuit. Frightened that the dog might come to grief, I asked Badri to call it back, but he said it would be all right for the dog was always chasing this particular animal, which he said had done a lot of damage to his young trees. The dog was now gaining on the *langur,* and when it got to within a few yards the *langur* whipped round, got the dog by the ears, and bit a lump off the side of its head. The wound was a very severe one, and by the time we had finished attending to it my tea and a plate of hot *puris* [unleavened bread fried in butter] were ready for me.

I had told Badri about the tree I intended sitting on, and when I returned to the kill he insisted on going with me accompanied by two men carrying materials for making a small *machan*. Badri and the two men had lived under the shadow of the man-eater for over a year and had no illusions about it, and when they saw that there were no trees near the kill— with the exception of the one I had selected—in which a *machan* could be built, they urged me not to sit up that night, on the assumption that the tiger would remove the kill and provide me with a more suitable place to sit up the following night. This was what I myself would have done if the tiger had not been a man-eater, but as it was I was disinclined to miss a chance which might not recur on the morrow, even if it entailed a little risk. There were bears in this forest and if

one of them smelt the kill any hope I had of getting a shot at
the tiger would vanish, for Himalayan bears are no respecters
of tigers and do not hesitate to appropriate their kills. Climbing into the tree, smothered as it was by the rose bush, was
a difficult feat, and after I had made myself as comfortable
as the thorn permitted and my rifle had been handed up to
me Badri and his men left, promising to return early next
morning.

I was facing the hill, with the ravine behind me. I was in
clear view of any animal coming down from above, but if the
tiger came from below, as I expected, it would not see me
until it got to the kill. The bullock, which was white, was
lying on its right side with its legs towards me, and at a distance of about fifteen feet. I had taken my seat at 4 p.m. and
an hour later a *kakar* started barking on the side of the ravine
two hundred yards below me. The tiger was on the move, and
having seen it the *kakar* was standing still and barking. For a
long time it barked and then it started to move away, the bark
growing fainter and fainter until the sound died away round
the shoulder of the hill. This indicated that after coming
within sight of the kill, the tiger had lain down. I had expected this to happen after having been told by Badri the reasons for the failures to shoot the tiger over a kill. I knew the
tiger would not be lying somewhere nearby with his eyes and
ears open, to make quite sure there were no human beings
near the kill, before he approached it. Minute succeeded long
minute; dusk came; objects on the hill in front of me became
indistinct and then faded out. I could still see the kill as a
white blur when a stick snapped at the head of the ravine and
stealthy steps came towards me, and then stopped immediately below. For a minute or two there was dead silence, and
then the tiger lay down on the dry leaves at the foot of the
tree.

Heavy clouds had rolled up near sunset and there was now
a black canopy overhead blotting out the stars. When the
tiger eventually got up and went to the kill, the night could

best be described as pitch black. Strain my eyes as I would I could see nothing of the white bullock, and still less of the tiger. On reaching the kill the tiger started blowing on it. In the Himalayas, and especially in the summer, kills attract hornets, most of which leave as the light fades but those that are too torpid to fly remain, and a tiger—possibly after bitter experience—blows off the hornets adhering to the exposed portion of the flesh before starting to feed. There was no need for me to hurry over my shot for, close though it was, the tiger would not see me unless I attracted its attention by some movement or sound. I can see reasonably well on a dark night by the light of the stars, but there were no stars visible that night nor was there a flicker of lightning in the heavy clouds. The tiger had not moved the kill before starting to eat, so I knew he was lying broadside on to me, on the right-hand side of the kill.

Owing to the attempts that had been made to shoot the tiger I had a suspicion that it would not come before dark, and it had been my intention to take what aim I could—by the light of the stars—and then move the muzzle of my rifle sufficiently for my bullet to go a foot or two to the right of the kill. But now that the clouds had rendered my eyes useless, I would have to depend on my ears (my hearing at that time was perfect). Raising the rifle and resting my elbows on my knees, I took careful aim at the sound the tiger was making, and while holding the rifle steady, turned my right ear to the sound, and then back again. My aim was a little too high, so, lowering the muzzle a fraction of an inch, I again turned my head and listened. After I had done this a few times and satisfied myself that I was pointing at the sound, I moved the muzzle a little to the right and pressed the trigger. In two bounds the tiger was up the twenty-foot bank. At the top there was a small bit of flat ground, beyond which the hill went up steeply. I heard the tiger on the dry leaves as far as the flat ground, and then there was silence. This silence could be interpreted to mean either that the tiger had died on reaching the flat ground or that it was unwounded. Keeping the rifle to my shoulder I listened intently for three or four minutes, and as there was no further sound I lowered the rifle. This movement was greeted by a deep growl from the top of the bank. So the tiger was unwounded, and had seen me. My seat on the tree had originally been about ten feet up but, as I had nothing solid to sit on, the rose bush had sagged under my weight and I was now possibly no more than eight feet above ground, with my dangling feet considerably lower. And a little above and some twenty feet from me a tiger that I had every reason to believe was a man-eater was growling deep down in his throat.

The near proximity of a tiger in daylight, even when it has not seen you, causes a disturbance in the blood stream. When the tiger is not an ordinary one, however, but a man-eater and the time is ten o'clock on a dark night, and you know the man-eater is watching you, the disturbance in the blood stream becomes a storm. I maintain that a tiger does not kill beyond its requirements, except under provocation. The tiger that was growling at me already had a kill that would last it for two or three days and there was no necessity for it to kill me. Even so, I had an uneasy feeling that on this occasion this particular tiger might prove an exception to the rule. Tigers will at times return to a kill after being fired at, but I knew this one would not do so. I also knew that in spite of my uneasy feeling I was perfectly safe so long as I did not lose my balance—I had nothing to hold on to—or go to sleep and fall off the tree. There was no longer any reason for me to deny myself a smoke, so I took out my cigarette case and as I lit a match I heard the tiger move away from the edge of the bank. Presently it came back and again growled. I had smoked three cigarettes, and the tiger was still with me, when it came on to rain. A few big drops at first and then a heavy downpour. I had put on light clothes when I started from Ramgarh that morning and in a few minutes I was wet to the skin, for there was not a leaf above me to diffuse the rain-drops. The tiger, I knew, would have hurried off to shelter under a tree or on the lee of a rock the moment the rain started. The rain came on at 11 p.m.; at 4 a.m. it stopped and the sky cleared. A wind now started to blow, to add to my discomfort, and where I had been cold before I was now frozen. When I get a twinge of rheumatism I remember that night and others like it, and am thankful that it is no more than a twinge.

Badri, good friend that he was, arrived with a man carrying a kettle of hot tea just as the sun was rising. Relieving me of my rifle the two men caught me as I slid off the tree, for my legs were too cramped to function. Then as I lay on the ground and drank the tea they massaged my legs and restored circulation. When I was able to stand, Badri sent his man off to light a fire in the guest house. I had never previously used my ears to direct a bullet and was interested to find that I had missed the tiger's head by only a few inches. The elevation had been all right but I had not moved the muzzle of the rifle far enough to the right, with the result that my bullet had struck the bullock six inches from where the tiger was eating.

The tea and the half-mile walk up to the road took all the creases out of me, and when we started down the mile-long track to Badri's orchard wet clothes and an empty stomach were my only discomfort. The track ran over red clay which the rain had made very slippery. In this clay were three tracks: Badri's and his man's tracks going up, and the man's tracks going down. For fifty yards there were only these three tracks in the wet clay, and then, where there was a bend in the track, a tigress had jumped down from the bank on the right and gone down the track on the heels of Badri's man. The footprints of the man and the pug-marks of the tigress showed that both had been travelling at a fast pace. There was nothing that Badri and I could do, for the man had a twenty-minute start of us, and if he had not reached the safety of the orchard he would long ere this have been beyond any help we could give him. With uneasy thoughts assailing us we made what speed we could on the slippery ground and were very relieved to find, on coming to a footpath from where the orchard and a number of men working it were visible, that the tigress had gone down the path while the man had carried on to the orchard. Questioned later, the man said he did not know that he had been followed by the tigress.

While drying my clothes in front of a roaring wood-fire in the guest house, I questioned Badri about the jungle into which the tigress had gone. The path which the tigress had taken, Badri told me, ran down into a deep and densely wooded ravine which extended down the face of a very steep hill, for a mile or more, to where it was met by another ravine coming down from the right. At the junction of the two ravines there was a stream and here there was an open patch of ground which, Badri said, commanded the exit of both ravines. Badri was of the opinion that the tigress would lie up for the day in the ravine into which we had every reason to believe she had gone, and as this appeared to be an ideal place for a beat, we decided to try this method of getting a shot at the tigress, provided we could muster sufficient men to carry out the beat. Govind Singh, Badri's head gardener, was summoned and our plan explained to him. Given until midday, Govind Singh said he could muster a gang of thirty men to do the beat, and in addition carry out his master's orders to gather five *maunds* [four hundred and ten pounds] of peas. Badri had an extensive vegetable garden in addition to his apple orchard and the previous evening he had received a telegram informing him that the price of marrowfat peas in the Naini Tal market had jumped to four annas [four pence] a pound. Badri was anxious to take advantage of this good price and his men were gathering the peas to be dispatched by pack pony that night, to arrive in Naini Tal for the early morning market.

After cleaning my rifle and walking round the orchard, I joined Badri at his morning meal—which had been put forward an hour to suit me—and at midday Govind produced his gang of thirty men. It was essential for someone to supervise the pea-pickers, so Badri decided to remain and send Govind to carry out the beat. Govind and the thirty men were local residents and knew the danger to be apprehended from the man-eater. However, after I had told them what I wanted them to do, they expressed their willingness to carry out my instructions. Badri was to give me an hour's start to enable me to search the ravine for the tigress and, if I failed to get a shot, to take up my position on the open ground near the stream. Govind was to divide his men into two parties, take charge of one party himself, and put a reliable man in charge of the other. At the end of the hour Badri was to fire a shot and the two parties were to set off, one on either side of the ravine, rolling rocks down, and shouting and clapping their hands. It all sounded as simple as that, but I had my doubts, for I have seen many beats go wrong.

Going up the track down which I had come that morning, I followed the path that the tigress had taken, only to find after I had gone a short distance that it petered out in a vast expanse of dense brushwood. Forcing my way through for several hundred yards I found that the hillside was cut up by a series of deep ravines and ridges. Going down a ridge which I thought was the right-hand boundary of the ravine to be beaten, I came to a big drop at the bottom of which the ravine on my left met a ravine coming down from the right, and at the junction of the two ravines there was a stream. While I was looking down and wondering where the open ground was on which I was to take my stand, I heard flies buzzing near me and on following the sound found the remains of a cow that had been killed about a week before. The marks on the animal's throat showed that it had been killed by a tiger. The tiger had eaten all of the cow, except a portion of the shoulders, and the neck and head. Without having any particular reason for doing so, I dragged the carcass to the edge and sent it crashing down the steep hill. After rolling for about a hundred yards the carcass fetched up in a little hollow a short distance from the stream. Working round to the left I found an open patch of ground on a ridge about three hundred yards from the hollow into which I had rolled the remains of the cow. The ground down here was very different from what I had pictured it to be. There was no place where I could stand to overlook the hillside that was to be beaten, and the tigress might break out anywhere without my seeing her. However, it was then too late to do anything, for Badri had fired the shot that was to let me know the beat had started. Presently, away in the distance, I heard men shouting. For a time I thought the beat was coming my way and then the sounds grew fainter and fainter until they eventually died away. An hour later I again heard the beaters. They were coming down the hill to my right, and when they were on a level with me I shouted to them to stop the beat and join me on the ridge. It was no one's fault that the beat had miscarried, for without knowing the ground and without previous preparation we had tried to beat with a handful of untrained men a vast area of dense brushwood that hundreds of trained men would have found it difficult to cope with.

The beaters had had a very strenuous time forcing their way through the brushwood, and while they sat in a bunch removing thorns from their hands and feet and smoking my cigarettes Govind and I stood facing each other, discussing his suggestion of carrying out a beat on the morrow in which every available man in Muktesar and the surrounding villages would take part. Suddenly, in the middle of a sentence, Govind stopped talking. I could see that something unusual had attracted his attention behind me, for his eyes narrowed and a look of incredulity came over his face. Swinging round I looked in the direction in which he was facing, and there, quietly walking along a field that had gone out of cultivation, was the tigress. She was about four hundred yards away on the hill on the far side of the stream, and was coming towards us.

When a tiger is approaching you in the forest—even when you are far from human habitations—thoughts course through your mind of the many things that can go wrong to spoil your chance of getting the shot, or the photograph, you are hoping for. On one occasion I was sitting on a hillside overlooking a game track, waiting for a tiger. The track led to a very sacred jungle shrine known as *Baram ka Than*. Baram is a jungle God who protects human beings and does not permit the shooting of animals in the area he watches over. The forest in the heart of which this shrine is situated is well stocked with game and is a favourite hunting ground of poachers for miles round, and of sportsmen from all parts of India. Yet, in a lifetime's acquaintance with that forest, I do not know of a single instance of an animal having been shot in the vicinity of the shrine. When therefore I set out that day to shoot a tiger that had been taking toll of our village buffaloes, I selected a spot a mile from Baram's shrine. I was in position, behind a bush, at 4 P.M. and an hour later a *sambhar* belled in the direction from which I was expecting the tiger. A little later and a little nearer to me a *kakar* started barking; the tiger was coming along the track near which I was sitting. The jungle was fairly open and consisted mostly of young *jamun* trees, two to three feet in girth. I caught sight of the tiger—a big male—when he was two hundred yards away. He was coming slowly and had reduced the distance between us to a hundred yards when I heard the swish of leaves, and on looking up saw that one of the *jamun* trees whose branches were interlaced with another was beginning to lean over. Very slowly the tree heeled over until it came in contact with another tree of the same species and of about the same size. For a few moments the second tree supported the weight of the first and then it, too, started to heel over. When the two trees were at an angle of about thirty degrees from the perpendicular they fetched up against a third and smaller tree. For a moment or two there was a pause, and then all three trees crashed to the ground. While watching the trees, which were only a few yards from me, I had kept an eye on the tiger. At the first sound of the leaves he had come to a halt and when the trees crashed to the ground he turned and, without showing any sign of alarm, went back in the direction from which he had come. What made the occurrence I had witnessed so unusual was that the trees were young and vigorous; that no rain had fallen recently to loosen their roots; that not a breath of air was stirring in the forest; and, finally, that the trees had fallen across the track leading to the shrine when the tiger had only another seventy yards to cover to give me the shot I was waiting for.

The chances of a shot being spoilt are greatly increased when the quarry is in an inhabited area in which parties of men may be travelling from one village to another or going to or from markets, or where shots may be fired to scare away *langurs* from apple orchards. The tigress still had three hundred yards to go to reach the stream, and two hundred yards of that was over open ground on which there was not a single tree or bush. The tigress was coming towards us at a slight angle and would see any movement we made, so there was nothing I could do but watch her, and no tigress had ever moved more slowly. She was known to the people of Muktesar as the lame tiger, but I could see no sign of her being lame. The plan that was forming in my head as I watched her was to wait until she entered the scrub jungle, and then run forward and try to get a shot at her either before or after she crossed the stream. Had there been sufficient cover between me and the point the tigress was making for, I would have gone forward as soon as I saw her and tried either to get a shot at her on the open ground or, failing that, intercept her at the stream. But unfortunately there was not sufficient cover to mask my movements, so I had to wait until the tigress entered the bushes between the open ground and the stream. Telling the men not to move or make a sound until I returned, I set off at a run as the tigress disappeared from view. The hill was steep and as I ran along the contour I came to a wild rose bush which extended up and down the hill for many yards. Through the middle of the bush there was a low tunnel, and as I bent down to run through it my hat was knocked off, and raising my head too soon at the end of the tunnel I was nearly dragged off my feet by the thorns that entered my head. The thorns of these wild roses are curved and very strong and as I was not able to stop myself some embedded themselves and broke off in my head—where my sister Maggie had difficulty in removing them when I got home—while others tore through the flesh. With little trickles of blood running down my face I continued to run until I approached the hollow into which I had rolled the partly-eaten kill from the hill above. This hollow was about forty yards long and thirty yards wide. The upper end of it where the kill was lying, the hill above the kill, and the further bank, were overgrown with dense brushwood. The lower half of the hollow and the bank on my side were free of bushes. As I reached the edge of the hollow and peered over, I heard a bone crack. The tigress had reached the hollow before me and, on finding the old kill, was trying to make up for the meal she had been deprived of the previous night.

If after leaving the kill, on which there was very little flesh, the tigress came out on to the open ground I would get a shot at her, but if she went up the hill or up the far bank I would not see her. From the dense brushwood in which I could hear the tigress a narrow path ran up the bank on my side and passed within a yard to my left, and a yard beyond the path there was a sheer drop of fifty feet into the stream below. I was considering the possibility of driving the tigress out of the brushwood on to the open ground by throwing a stone on to the hill above her, when I heard a sound behind me. On looking round I saw Govind standing behind me with my hat in his hand. At that time no European in India went about without a hat, and having seen mine knocked off by the rose bush Govind had retrieved it and brought it to me. Near us there was a hole in the hill. Putting my finger to my lips I got Govind by the arm and pressed him into the hole. Sitting on his hunkers with his chin resting on his drawn-up knees, hugging my hat, he just fitted into the hole and looked a very miserable object, for he could hear the tigress crunching bones a few yards away. As I straightened up and resumed my position on the edge of the bank, the tigress stopped eating. She had either seen me or, what was more probable, she had not found the old kill to her liking. For a long minute there was no movement or sound, and then I caught sight of her. She had climbed up the opposite bank, and was now going along the top of it towards the hill. At this point there was a number of six-inch-thick poplar saplings, and I could only see the outline of the tigress as she went through them. With the forlorn hope that my bullet would miss the saplings and find the tigress I threw up my rifle and took a hurried shot. At my shot the tigress whipped round, came down the bank, across the hollow, and up the path on my side, as hard as she could go. I did not know, at the time, that my bullet had struck a sapling near her head, and that she was blind of one eye. So what looked like a very determined charge might only have been a frightened animal running away from danger, for in that restricted space she would not have known from what direction the report of my rifle had come. Be that as it may, what I took to be a wounded and a very angry tigress was coming straight at me; so, waiting until she was two yards away, I leant forward and with great good luck managed to put the remaining bullet in the rifle into the hollow where her neck joined her shoulder. The impact of the heavy .500 bullet deflected her just sufficiently for her to miss my left shoulder, and her impetus carried her over the fifty-foot drop into the stream below, where she landed with a great splash. Taking a step forward I looked over the edge and saw the tigress lying submerged in a pool with her feet in the air, while the water in the pool reddened with her blood.

Govind was still sitting in the hole, and at a sign he joined me. On seeing the tigress he turned and shouted to the men on the ridge, "The tiger is dead. The tiger is dead." The thirty men on the ridge now started shouting, and Badri on hearing them got hold of his shotgun and fired off ten rounds. These shots were heard at Muktesar and in the surrounding villages, and presently men from all sides were converging on the stream. Willing hands drew the tigress from the pool, lashed her to a sapling and carried her in triumph to Badri's orchard. Here she was put down on a bed of straw for all to see, while I went to the guest house for a cup of tea. An hour later by the light of hand lanterns, and with a great crowd of men standing round, among whom were several sportsmen from Muktesar, I skinned the tigress. It was then that I found she was blind of one eye and that she had some fifty porcupine quills, varying in length from one to nine inches, embedded in the arm and under the pad of her right foreleg. By ten o'clock my job was finished, and declining Badri's very kind invitation to spend the night with him I climbed the hill in company with the people who had come down from Muktesar, among whom were my two men carrying the skin. On the open ground in front of the post office the skin was spread out for the Postmaster and his friends to see. At midnight I lay down in the dak bungalow reserved for the public, for a few hours' sleep. Four hours later I was on the move again and at midday I was back in my home at Naini Tal after an absence of seventy-two hours.

The shooting of a man-eater gives one a feeling of satisfaction. Satisfaction at having done a job that badly needed doing. Satisfaction at having out-manoeuvred, on his own ground, a very worthy antagonist. And, greatest satisfaction of all, at having made a small portion of the earth safe for a brave little girl to walk on.

For decades, the Bengal tiger, one of nature's crowning achievements, was an endangered species. Over the last twenty years, preservation efforts have secured the tiger's place in the world, although it will never enjoy the numbers it once did. The likes of Captain Jim Corbett, white hunter and champion of the British Raj, have since become a quaint, almost mythical symbol of an era now lost in time.

The great white hunter emerged in British colonies through demand and opportunity. The "slayers of dragons," as white hunters were once referred to in India, became heroic figures. They had guns and the expertise to use them effectively. The need to eliminate man-eaters provided these men the chance to gain the experience and confidence to slay dragons. Reputation and time made them legends and, to be sure, Captain Jim Corbett is a legend.

As this and other attack stories attest, whenever a hunter tracks a lethal carnivore, he commits to a kind of ultimate confidence game. Even Captain Jim Corbett would not do this, we assume, unless he felt that experience and a world-class rifle gave him the advantage. Most stories, however, reveal that each man-eater is a new experience for the hunter and that a rifle is often little more than a prop in a drama of wits, nerve, and spontaneous resourcefulness. Again and again, big-game hunters' accounts emphasize the *unpredictability* of the game. Experience will teach what a predator might do, but until the moment of attack, the hunter never really knows. But the best of the white hunters knew with certainty that their nerve and skill would not be compromised by the spectacle of, say, a lunging tiger. These men were no less fearful than others, but they had faced their own fears and found, remarkably, an ability to get the job done in the most extreme circumstances. In this sense, the campaigns of hunters like Captain Jim Corbett are a metaphor of promise for every person who has ever faced fear and found the courage to act.

J.L.

---- ◆ ----

Assassino

Peter Hathaway Capstick

During the years that he had been on his crusade of slaughter, Assassino had earned the reputation as a "devil-cat," much the same status successful man-eaters in Africa and Asia are awarded. No bullet could harm him, the thinking went, nor could any man kill him. Anybody who hunted him lost all his dogs and never got so much as a glimpse of his anthracite and amber hide. After killing an estimated 400 head of cattle to the south of the Xarayes, for some reason he became inactive for several months before resurfacing near the Fazenda Descalvados, a large ranch in the Xarayes Pantanal of Brazil. It may have been that he was injured in a territorial battle or was sick for a while; no one knows.

Alexander "Sasha" Siemel refused to hunt Assassino, although begged to do so by ranchers on several occasions. He was only too aware, as a professional, that to try to hunt the big jaguar with his hounds would be a death sentence for them, skilled though they were. And now, without his lead dog Valente, who might have stood some chance, there was no hope for it. But this decision was made before Assassino killed Jose Ramos.

It was Ramos himself who had ridden into Siemel's camp near Ilha do Cara Cara, his horse lathered and his clothes crusty with sweat. Not taking time to dismount, he implored Siemel to come with his dogs to hunt Assassino, who had killed twelve of his small herd.

Siemel turned him down flat. He would as soon send the fox terrier pup as his jaguar dogs for all the chance they would have. Jose Ramos, desperate, begged again, but the most Siemel could promise was that he would go after the cat if he saw him or knew he was close by. With resignation, Ramos swore to go after Assassino himself. He would kill or be killed. Little did he realize.

Within two day's of Ramos' visit, Siemel noticed a tall, dense column of vultures circling over the marshes some miles off. Suspecting one of Assassino's calling cards, he investigated and soon found the mangled body of a marsh deer, the carcass badly ripped by claws and teeth but the meat uneaten. Incredibly, as he went on with the dogs in close control, five marsh deer in all were found executed by the assassin cat, the spoor of his huge pug marks unmistakable. Not one ounce of meat had been eaten from any of the bodies except by the urubi. Assassino was back in top form.

At the fifth kill, Ravioso lost control and ran off on the scent of the jaguar, Siemel quickly collaring the other dogs lest they take up the deadly trail as well. Clenching his teeth, Siemel listened to the bass bawling of the lead dog through the long grass, knowing what he would hear soon. It came as a piercing canine scream of agony that stopped abruptly as a slammed door. Assassino had won again.

Siemel was at a loss as to how to hunt this insane cat through the dense cover of the marshes. Back at camp, having buried the tattered remains of Ravioso, he thought back over the jaguar's career, realizing the apparent impossibility of trying to run down the big cat without dogs, at the same time knowing that to expose his pack was as good as shooting them. For hours he pondered the problem. His rifle would be useless in the heavy grass; only the spear could draw the life blood of the cat at such suicidally close quarters. But, he thought, even with the loss of Raivoso, possibly he could use the dogs to get close enough to the jaguar to deal with it. He was still wrestling with the problem the next morning when the thud of Maria Ramos' horse galloping into camp set little Tupi into a paroxysm of barking.

Maria was a wreck. Half-hysterical and bush-torn, she poured out all she knew; that Jose had gone after Assassino and only the claw-torn horse had returned with blood on the saddle. To a junglewise tigrero like Siemel, it was like reading a newspaper headline. There was nothing to do but go now and try to find whatever might be left of Jose Ramos. Siemel took four leashed dogs, two new ones called Amigo and Leon joining with Vinte and Pardo, and tied the fox terrier to one of the hut poles so he would not follow. Maria led the way along the river to the place where she said Jose had cut off the trail, refusing when Siemel tried to get her to ride home. She was a woman of the pantanal and insisted on coming.

A mile ahead, the green capao stood like a beacon over the ocean of grass, a strange, verdant projection like a lichen-covered rock in a tropical sea. Far above, speck-like vultures volplaned and circled.

Jose Ramos lay as Assassino had left him, a mass of torn meat lying on its face. As Siemel rolled the corpse over in a loud whine of flies, Maria fainted and fell from her horse. She did not now argue when sent back to the ranch.

The sign was clear: Deep scars marked the spot from which the jaguar had leaped, and blackening speckles of blood freckled the grass stems around the hoof marks. Some yards away lay the unfired percussion gun. Siemel looked around him. If Assassino had knocked a man from his horse once, he would do it again. Also, there was no way to spear-fight effectively from horseback. Dismounting, he tied the animal to a tree in a small clearing and unsheathed his zagaya blade. A pistol—the ubiquitous Smith and Wesson .38 Special revolver, the Brazilian standard against which all other handguns were judged—was in his belt holster. Years later, while spear-fighting a jaguar, Siemel would manage to shoot himself in the leg with this very pistol. In any case, the .38 Special cartridge is of little value against a charging jaguar and was carried for delivering the coup de grace—the brain shot. On a hunch, he also took his bow and two arrows, in case he had the opportunity of provoking a charge with them.

A very simple plan—Siemel decided that the cat was probably still quite close, and, by releasing the dogs and running after them at speed, there was a possibility that he might throw the jaguar's ambush tactics off. Yes, if he could keep up, maybe there was a chance. He let slip the dogs.

After ten minutes of running through the marsh grass, the vocal bedlam of the dogs ever farther ahead, he knew that he had been wrong. The death shriek of Padro, the leader, sounded over the plain and was followed in less than a minute by the screech of the disembowelled Vinte. Within 450 yards, Assassino killed all four dogs in his classic ambush pattern. His lungs of fire, Siemel was sick with fury at finding the last one, Leon, in an opening in the capao. And then another bark filtered through the bush and caught his ear. It was the fox terrier, Tupi, who had chewed through his tether and followed his master's scent.

As the little dog ran by, barking insanely at the cat smell, Siemel slammed his heel over the trailing end of the broken tether, flipping Tupi over as the line tautened in a full run. As the pet yelped in surprise, that same moment there was a rustle of heavy movement just across the clearing. Then ominous silence. Carefully, Siemel laid his spear at his feet and nocked an arrow. Without a glance down, he stepped on the little dog's foot, making it shriek with startled pain.

It worked. Across the opening a few stalks of grass

twitched. In a single fluid movement, Siemel came to full draw, and his arrow hissed blindly into the tangle as Tupi began to bark again. The thug! of the arrow told Siemel he had touched the jaguar, and there was a flurry of movement through the curtain of grass. Scant seconds ticked mutely by in time with his heaving chest as he sighted his last shaft and sent it whipping into the cover. Would the confusion of the barking dog and the flash of the arrows bring the charge be needed? The answer appeared in a blur of streaking motion as Assassino, a broken-off shaft protruding form the bunched muscles of his shoulder, ran for a low scrub tree out of pure instinct. He was nearly there when he saw Siemel.

The man gulped involuntarily when he saw the jaguar's tremendous size as the cat stopped and then stood glowering at Siemel across a thirty-yard open space. The zagaya in position, the spearman realized that he would never again have a fight like this one, very possibly because he would not be alive for the next one. He had none of the advantages of the dogs to break the concentration of the jaguar, to keep him off balance. Furious with pain in his shoulder, the monster cat would be completely unpredictable in his next attack. The killer cat measured the man, stalking back and forth with guttural growls as if caged, punctuated with screaming roars that fluttered Siemel's guts. Every sense locked on the cat, Siemel began to move slowly in, edging closer, pushing for the charge. Both man and jaguar were searching for an opening. The cat's came first.

It was just the airy flutter of wings, the flap of an urubi vulture settling into a tree above him. But it was enough. The terrible strain broke Siemel's all-important concentration, and he committed the fatal sin of glancing away from the jaguar. In a microsecond, it saw its chance and launched itself straight at the spearman. Off balance, Siemel lunged and pivoted at the same time, the foot-long forged-steel spearhead catching Assassino a lucky slice on the neck as the mottled mass of golden-sheathed muscle hurtled by. A giant, talon studded paw glanced off Siemel's right shoulder, knocking him down like a flung doll. In that moment he should have been a dead man.

Somehow, probably because of the shock of the neck wound, the cat was also thrown off balance. Siemel gained the second he needed to roll to the side and scramble to his knees, the spearblade once more leveled and weaving for a thrust. As lithe as any cat, Siemel regained his feet. He could feel his strength flowing away like sweat, but Assassino was also showing some effect of the heavily bleeding neck wound. Mere feet between them, the two fighters stood panting, eyes locked, for what seemed to Siemel an eternity. He knew that if he could drive the blade home once more, he would win. The question was whether he could stand up to the charge that would make that thrust possible. He did not have long to ponder the question. As if reading his mind, through the blue eyes, the jaguar gave a last terrific roar and exploded straight at Siemel.

It was so fast and from so close range that Siemel nearly did not manage to lift the spear point in time. As the irresistible impact slammed through the thick shaft of louro wood, he saw that the blade had caught the throat too high, and a thrill of horror race over him; so close were the raking claws that he was sure he had held the shaft too far forward. As he had seen Joaquin Guato do, he pushed forward hard, withdrawing the spear, and in the same motion plunged it deep into the chest. With the last of his draining strength, he pinned the jaguar down, the cutting steel buried near the heart. Assassino fought madly, its lashing claws deeply lacerating the spear shaft, scoring the wood as Siemel drove his full weight down. As the tip of the blade passed completely through the chest and grated against the ground on the far side despite the flesh-buried cross-stop, the paw strokes slowed and, with a great shudder, stopped. How long he leaned on the zagaya shaft, Sasha Siemel did not know. He didn't know that Assassino was dead, and he was alive.

Anger, terror, necessity, and a willingness to test his own mortality transformed Sasha Siemel into a predator and led him into the tangled brush. He knew that a man-eating jaguar is a formidable opponent, unsurpassed for stealth and savagery. A lion or tiger will usually attack one victim and stay at it until the prey is dead, but jaguars are more like leopards, able to strike at a group, slashing one after the other until all are disabled. Siemel knew that the jaguar might drop from a tree or come out of heavy cover with such speed and ferocity that a brace of shotguns would still be inadequate protection. With its natural camouflage, the cat could crouch unseen only a few yards away. Many times Siemel had witnessed jaguars strike before a shot could be fired. But he entered the thicket anyway, armed with a bow and arrow and a spear.

If you didn't think Siemel mad when he entered the scrub, you may have been convinced he was when he stepped on his dog's leg to raise a yelp and, in effect, said to one of nature's deadliest creatures, "Here I am. Let's have at it." What kind of primal faith or belief did Siemel tap into that told him he was not signing his own death certificate? What good is a spear and a bow and arrow against a crazed jaguar? Evidently, they are good enough. But was it his weapons or his faith and belief that saw him through? Perhaps Sasha Siemel shows us that the belief that becomes true is the one that allows us the best use of our strength and the means to translate it into action.

J.L.

Come Quick! I'm Being Eaten by a Bear

Cynthia Dusel-Bacon

The summer of 1977 was my third summer in the Yukon-Tanana Upland of Alaska, doing geologic field mapping for the Alaskan Geology Branch of the U.S. Geological Survey. I began working for the USGS in the summer of 1975, making helicopter-assisted traverses in the highest terrain of the 6,000-square-mile Big Delta quadrangle.

The second summer, the project chief and I found it necessary to map the geology by backpacking, usually a week at a time, because our budget did not provide for helicopter expenses. Then, in 1977 we were again funded for helicopter transport, after an initial month of backpacking. All five geologists in our group, after being transported by air to the field area, usually mapped alone. Although I was concerned about the added risk brought about by working alone, I did enjoy the solitude and the opportunity to be by myself in a beautiful wilderness area.

Every summer in the upland area we saw bears. The first

one I saw was walking slowly along on the far side of a small mountain meadow. I froze. It didn't see me and disappeared into the forest. Another time I was walking through a spruce forest and saw a black bear moving through the trees some distance away. Again, I apparently was not noticed. The second summer while I was backpacking, I encountered a small black bear coming along the trail toward me. I had been busy looking down at the ground for chips of rock when I heard a slight rustling sound. I looked up to see the bear about 40 feet in front of me. Startled, it turned around and ran off in the other direction, crashing through the brush as it left the trail. This particular experience reassured me that what I had heard about black bears being afraid of people was, in fact, true.

During the third summer, I saw my first grizzly, but only from the air. Although other members of our field party had seen them on the ground, I felt fortunate to have encountered only black bears. Grizzlies were generally considered to be more unpredictable and dangerous.

I had hiked through the bush unarmed each summer, because our project chief felt that guns would add more danger to an encounter than they might prevent. A wounded, angry bear would probably be more dangerous than a frightened one. Consequently, she had strongly discouraged us from carrying any kind of firearm. We all carried walkie-talkie radios to keep in constant touch with one another and with our base camp. Everyone was well aware of the dangers of surprising bears or getting between a mother and her cubs. Whenever I was doing field mapping, I always attempted to make noise as I walked, so that I would alert any bears within hearing distance and give them time to run away from me. For two summers this system worked perfectly.

In the summer of 1977 we were scheduled to complete the reconnaissance mapping of the Big Delta quadrangle. Since it is such a large area, we needed helicopter transportation to finish by mid-September. At about 8:30 A.M., August 13,

1977, Ed Spencer, our helicopter pilot, dropped me off near the top of a rocky, brush-covered ridge approximately 60 miles southeast of Fairbanks. I was dressed in khaki work pants and a cotton shirt. I wore sturdy hiking boots and carried a rucksack. In the right outside pocket of my pack I carried a light lunch of baked beans, canned fruit, fruit juice, and a few crackers. My walkie-talkie was in the left outside pocket, complete with covering flap, strap, and buckle. I was to take notes on the geology, collect samples with the geologist's hammer I carried on my belt, record my location on the map, and stow the samples in my rucksack. Standard safety procedure called for me to make radio contact with the other geologists and with our base camp several times during the day at regular intervals. The radio in camp, about 80 miles south of the mapping area, was being monitored by the wife of the helicopter pilot. I was to be picked up by helicopter at the base of the four-mile-long ridge on a gravel bar of the river at the end of the day.

After noticing, with unexpected pleasure, that I was going to be able to use a narrow trail that had been bulldozed along the crest of the ridge, I started off downhill easily, on the trail that passed through tangles of birch brush and over rough, rocky slopes. The ridge was in one of the more accessible parts of the quadrangle. There are a few small cabins about five to ten miles downstream along the Salcha River, and a short landing strip for airplanes is about five miles from the ridge. Fishermen sometimes venture this far up the river too, so bears in the area probably have seen human beings on occasion. That particular morning I wasn't expecting to see bears at all; the hillside was so rocky and so dry and tangled with brush that it just didn't seem like bear country. I felt that if I were to see a bear at all that day, it would likely be at the end of the day, down along the river bar and adjoining woods.

I descended the ridge slowly for several hundred yards, moving from one outcrop of rock to another, breaking off samples and putting them in my pack. I stopped at one large outcrop to break off an interesting piece and examine it. A sudden loud crash in the undergrowth below startled me and I looked around just in time to see a black bear rise up out of the brush about 10 feet away.

My first thought was, "Oh, no! A bear. I'd better do the right thing." My next thought was one of relief: "It's only a black bear, and a rather small one at that." Nevertheless, I decided to get the upper hand immediately and scare it away.

I shouted at it, face to face, in my most commanding tone of voice. "Shoo! Get out of here, bear! Go on! Get away!" The bear remained motionless and glared back at me. I clapped my hands and yelled even louder. But even that had no effect. Instead of turning and running away into the brush, the bear began slowly walking, climbing toward my level, watching me steadily. I waved my arms, clapped and yelled even more wildly. I began banging on the outcrop with my hammer, making all the noise I could to intimidate the bear.

I took a step back, managing to elevate myself another foot or so in an attempt to reach a more dominant position. By this time the bear had reached the trail I was on and was slightly uphill from me. It slowly looked up the hill in the direction from which I had come and then stared back at me again. I knew that in this moment the bear was trying to decide whether it should retreat from me or attack. Suddenly the bear darted around behind the outcrop and behind me. My next sensation was that of being struck a staggering blow from behind. I felt myself being thrown forward, and I landed face down on the ground, with my arms outstretched.

I froze, not instinctively but deliberately, remembering that playing dead was supposed to cause an attacking bear to lose interest and go away. Instead of hearing the bear crashing off through the brush, though, I felt the sudden piercing pain of the bear's teeth biting deep into my right shoulder. I felt myself being shaken with tremendous, irresistible power by teeth deep in my shoulder. After playing dead for several minutes, I came to the horrible realization that the bear had no intention of abandoning its prey.

"I've got to get my radio in the pack. I've got to get a call out," I thought.

My left arm was free, so I tried to reach behind myself to the left outside pocket of my rucksack to get at the walkie-talkie. My heart sank as I discovered that the buckled flap on the pocket prevented me from getting out my radio. My movement caused the bear to start a new flurry of biting and tearing at the flesh of my upper right arm again. I was completely conscious of feeling my flesh torn, teeth against bone, but the sensation was more of numb horror at what was happening to me than of specific reaction to each bite. I remember thinking, "Now I'm never going to be able to call for help. I'm dead unless this bear decides to leave me alone."

The bear had no intention of leaving me alone. After chewing on my right shoulder, arm, and side repeatedly, the bear began to bite my head and tear at my scalp. As I heard the horrible crunching sound of the bear's teeth biting into my skull, I realized it was all too hopeless. I remember thinking, "This has got to be the worst way to go." I knew it would be a slow death because my vital signs were all still strong. My fate was to bleed to death. I thought, "Maybe I should just shake my head and get the bear to do me in quickly."

All of a sudden, the bear clamped its jaws into me and began dragging me by the right arm down the slope through the brush. I was dragged about 20 feet or so before the bear stopped to rest, panting in my ear. It began licking at the blood that was now running out of a large wound under my right arm. Again the bear pulled me along the ground, over rocks and through brush, stopping frequently to rest, and chewing at my arm. Finally it stopped, panting heavily. It had been dragging me and my 20-pound pack—a combined weight of about 150 pounds—for almost half an hour over rocks and through brush. Now it walked about four feet away and sat down to rest, still watching me intently.

Here, I thought, might be a chance to save myself yet—if only I could get at that radio. Slowly I moved my left arm, which was on the side away from the bear, and which was still undamaged, behind me to get at that pack buckle. But this time the pocket, instead of being latched tight, was wide open—the buckle probably was torn off by the bear's clawing or from being dragged over the rocks. I managed to reach down into the pocket and pull out the radio. Since my right arm was now completely numb and useless, I used my left hand to stealthily snap on the radio switch, pull up two of the three segments of the antenna, and push in the button activating the transmitter. Holding the radio close to my mouth, I said as loudly as I dared, "Ed, this is Cynthia. Come quick, I'm being eaten by a bear." I said "eaten" because I was convinced that the bear wasn't just mauling me or playing with me, but was planning to consume me. I was its prey, and it had no intention of letting me escape.

I repeated my message and then started to call out some more information. "Ed, I'm just down the hill from where you left me off this morning . . ." but I got no further. By this time the bear had risen to its feet; it bounded quickly over to me and savagely attacked my left arm, knocking the radio out of my hand. I screamed in pain as I felt my good arm being torn and mangled by claws and teeth.

It was then I realized I had done all I could do to save my life. I had no way of knowing whether anyone had even heard my calls. I really doubted it, since no static or answering sound from anyone trying to call had come back over the receiver. I knew I hadn't taken time to extend the antenna completely. I knew I was down in a ravine, with many ridges between me and a receiving set. I knew there was really no chance for me. I was doomed. So I screamed as the bear tore at my arm, figuring that it was going to eat me anyway and there was no longer any reason to try to control my natural reactions. I remember that the bear then began sniffing around my body, down my calves, up my thighs. I could read the bear's mind as it tried to decide whether it should open up new wounds or continue on the old ones.

I didn't dare look around at what was happening—my eyes were fixed upon the dirt and leaves on the ground only inches below my face. Then I felt a tearing at the pack on my back, and heard the bear begin crunching cans in its teeth—cans I had brought for my lunch. This seemed to occupy its attention for a while; at least it left my arms alone and gave me a few moments to focus my mind on my predicament.

"Is this how I'm going to go?" I remember marveling at how clear my mind was, how keen my senses were. All I could think of as I lay there on my stomach, with my face down in the dry grass and dirt and that merciless, blood-thirsty animal holding me down, was how much I wanted to live and how much I wanted to go back to Charlie, my husband of five months, and how tragic it would be to end it all three days before I turned thirty-one.

It was about ten minutes, I think, before I heard the faint sound of a helicopter in the distance. It came closer and then seemed to circle, as if making a pass, but not directly over me. Then I heard the helicopter going away, leaving me. What had gone wrong? Was it just a routine pass to transfer one of the other geologists to a different ridge, or to go to a gas cache to refuel and not an answer to my call for help? Had no one heard my call?

The bear had not been frightened by the sound of the helicopter. Having finished with the contents of my pack, it began to tear again at the flesh under my right arm. Then I heard the helicopter coming back, circling, getting closer. Being flat on my face, with both arms now completely without feeling, I kicked my legs to show whoever was up above me that I was still alive. This time, however, I was certain that I was to be rescued because the pilot hovered directly over me. But again I heard the helicopter suddenly start away over the ridge. In a few seconds all was silent; it was an agonizing silence. I couldn't believe it. For some reason they'd left me for the second time.

Suddenly I felt, or sensed, that the bear was not beside me. The sound of the chopper had frightened it away. Again—for about ten minutes—I waited in silence. Then I heard the helicopter coming over the ridge again, fast and directly toward me. In a few seconds the deafening, beautiful sound was right over me. I kicked my legs again and heard the helicopter move up toward the crest of the ridge for what I was now sure was a landing. Finally I heard the engine shut down, then voices, and people calling out. I yelled back to direct them to where I was lying. But the birch brush was thick, and with my khaki work pants and gray pack I was probably difficult to see lying on the ground among the rocks.

Ed was the first to spot me, and he called the two women geologists down the slope to help him. Together they managed to carry me up the hill and lift me up into the back seat of the helicopter. I remember the feeling of relief and thankfulness that swept over me when I found myself in that helicopter, going up and away over the mountain. I knew that my mind was clear and my breathing was good and my insides were all intact. All I had to do was keep cool and let the doctors fix me up. Deep down, though, I knew the extent of my injuries and knew that I had been too badly hurt for my body to ever be the same again.

They flew me to Fort Greeley army base in Delta Junction, about an hour's trip. There emergency measures were taken to stabilize my condition. I was given blood and probably some morphine to deaden the pain. An hour or so later I was flown up to the army hospital in Fairbanks and taken immediately into surgery. For the first time that day I lost consciousness—under the anesthesia.

My left arm had to be amputated above the elbow, about halfway between elbow and shoulder, because most of the flesh had been torn from my forearm and elbow. To try to save my right arm, which had not been so badly chewed, the doctors took a vein out of my left thigh and grafted it from underneath my badly damaged right arm, through the torn upper arm, and out to my lower arm. This vein became an artery to keep the blood circulating through my forearm and hand. Four surgeons continued working on me for about five hours, late into the evening. They also did some "debriding"—that is, removing hopelessly damaged tissue and cleaning the lacerated wounds of leaves, sticks, and dirt. I stayed at Fairbanks overnight and then was flown out at 3:00 P.M. Sunday for San Francisco.

By this time our branch chief had managed to notify Charlie, also a geologist for the U.S. Geological Survey, of my accident. Both were waiting for me when I arrived at the San Francisco airport at 1:00 A.M. Monday. I was taken immediately by ambulance to Stanford Hospital and put in the intensive-care ward.

Then began the vain attempts to save my right arm. For more than a week I held every hope that the vein graft was going to work. But a blood clot developed in the transplanted artery and circulation stopped. The pulse that had been felt in the right wrist and the warmth in my fingers disappeared and the whole arm became cold. Although another amputation was clearly going to be necessary, the doctors felt they should wait until a clearer line between good tissue and bad tissue became evident. Then they would amputate up to this point and save the rest.

But before that line appeared, I began to run a very high temperature. Fearing that the infected and dying arm was now endangering my life, the doctors took me into the operating room, found the tissue in my arm to be dead almost to the top of my shoulder, and removed the entire arm. Not even a stump of that arm could be saved.

As if this was not trouble enough, my side underneath the right shoulder had been opened up by the bear when it tore out and consumed the lymph glands under my right arm.

This area was raw and extremely susceptible to infection. It eventually would have to be covered by skin grafts, skin stripped from my own body. But before the skin graft could be done, new tissue would have to be regenerated in the wound to cover the exposed muscle and bone. I stayed in the hospital for weeks, absorbing nourishing fluids and antibiotics intravenously and eating high-protein meals of solid foods. Slowly, new flesh grew back to fill the hole, and the plastic surgeon was able to graft strips of skin taken from my right thigh to cover the raw flesh under my right shoulder. The thigh skin was laid on in strips like rolls of sod, kept clean and open to the air for many days, until it "took." These operations hospitalized me for a total of six weeks.

I am determined to lead as normal a life as possible. I know that there are certain limitations I can't get around, having to rely on artificial arms. But I'm certainly going to do the best I can with all that I have left. And that's a lot.

———————◆———————

We're all bothered by the notion that life might take a bottom turn and reduce us to victims. And from the safety of an armchair it's easy to beg and scream at Cynthia Dusel-Bacon to do something, *anything,* but play dead while a bear tears at her. But how would we fare if confronted by a feral beast? How could she have known that statistics show convincingly that, when a bear attacks, the victim who fights back is likely to fare better than one who plays dead?

During her weeks in the hospital, Dusel-Bacon had ample time to review her experience and ponder why the bear had attacked. She narrowed her conclusions:

> The bear may have been asleep in the bush and I startled it; it may have seen me as a threat, not only to itself, but also to any offspring that might have been nearby; or it was very hungry.

Regarding the first possibility, which I believe is the most likely one, the bear may have been asleep in the brush and woke startled when it heard me hammering on rocks. It should have had plenty of time to collect its wits, however, as it stared at me and circled me before charging. Although the terrain seemed rather unsuited for a comfortable lair—large, rectangular blocks of broken-off rubble covered the ground and were almost covered by birch brush—such a hidden spot may have seemed ideal to the bear.

It is also possible that the bear was instinctively fearful for the safety of a cub in the area. I never saw any other bear that day, but the helicopter pilot, after he left me at the Fort Greeley hospital, went with Fish and Game officials to find the bear that had attacked me so that it could be checked for rabies. They found and shot what they believed to be the guilty one. They reported the presence of a one-year-old cub in the area, but left it to take care of itself. If the mother encountered a strange creature in its territory and simultaneously noticed the absence of its cub, it could have reacted violently, out of fear for its cub. That I saw no cub suggests the possibility that the mother bear didn't either and may have felt, in sudden panic, that I had something to do with its disappearance.

The third possibility—that the bear was extremely hungry—could have been a factor, too. The postmortem analysis of the bear's stomach revealed only a few berries and some "unidentifiable substance," which may have been parts of me. I hadn't noticed any blueberry patches on the ridge, so the bear could have been tired of hunting for berries and decided to try for larger game, since it came upon me, either unexpectedly or deliberately, at a distance of only 10 feet.

One fact is certain: that bear wanted me for dinner. Once it tasted my flesh and blood, it did not intend to let me get away.

J.L.

I Hoped It Would Finish Me Quickly

Hugh Edwards

Putting one foot in front of the other was something Val Plumwood did well.

Bushwalking was an enjoyment for her and it fitted in naturally with her occupation as a lecturer in environmental philosophy at Macquarie University in Sydney, Australia.

She found that while she walked, her mind worked better than it did when she was sitting at a desk. Walking and thinking, thinking and walking, allowed her to observe environmental problems at first hand in the most pleasant and effective way.

From the time she was a young woman she took comfortable strides through the escarpment country of southern New South Wales. She loved the smell of eucalyptus and the sound of bird songs. She built her own house of stone there in the bush, five kilometers from the nearest neighbor.

"That's not to say I'm a hermit who doesn't like people's company. I do, and often seek it out. But sometimes I do like to be on my own. I'm very comfortable with myself and I enjoy my own company." She called the house Plumwood Mountain, after the Plumwood, a beautiful rainforest tree which grows there.

Val Plumwood did most things in a wholehearted fashion. Her bushwalks were no casual strolls to the bottom of the garden. In a motorized age when most city dwellers consider a kilometer walk from a concrete park an epic of endurance, she backpacked for days at a time. Some of her "walks" were as long as six days with groups of other walkers. She would spend up to four days on her own, walking and camping out overnight, enjoying the bushland solitude, the smell of earth and trees, and the sweet and secret sounds that town folk seldom hear.

Without realizing it, Val Plumwood was actually in training for a day when she would need all those reserves of physical strength. All her accumulated determination, simply to stay alive.

When she went to Kakadu National Park in the Northern Territory in February 1985, she had no particularly strong thoughts about crocodiles. They were part of the environment and they were protected—that was good.

"But they weren't in my specific field of interests. I was far more concerned with birds and I didn't even expect to have anything to do with crocodiles. So far as a wild animal risk went, I'd given much more thought to buffalo, creatures I expected I might bump into on a bushwalk and which can sometimes be dangerous."

Crocodiles were a part of the water and not a part of her expectations.

Val Plumwood stayed in a privately owned caravan at the park ranger base at the East Alligator River. "It wasn't official accommodation, but was arranged by a friend. I appreciated it."

About February 10, she completed a three-day bushwalk in the Mt. Brockman area. A stimulating experience. "It was really hot—quite different from what I was used to. But the Kakadu escarpment country is so beautiful. It surprises and delights you at every corner."

When she finished the walk Val Plumwood was probably as fit as she had ever been in her life.

Birds had always fascinated her. She spent a good deal of time in previous summers working on forest bird-breeding studies in New South Wales. She wanted naturally to see some of the Kakadu bird life and asked the advice of one of the rangers on the best places to study the water birds. Kakadu is a feathered paradise and a joy for those who like to watch birds. On the floodplains and billabongs there are magpie geese in thousands, flocks of pelicans and armies of ibis. As well as herons, egrets, brolgas and magnificent solitary jabiru storks, more than a third of Australia's bird species are found in Kakadu.

Her friend, who worked in the area, suggested she take a fiberglass Canadian canoe moored close to the ranger station. It was a good way to get close to the birds and allowed access to swampy areas difficult to reach on foot or by conventional boat.

"It seemed a good idea at the time," Val Plumwood recalls. "Canoes weren't a strong part of my experience. But it was easy to handle. It was about 14 feet long and there was no problem about balance. As canoes went it was a substantial sort of craft.

"The thinking at the time was that crocodiles didn't attack people in boats and though the thought did vaguely cross my mind it wasn't a serious worry. After all, a lot of people had been using it."

In fact Canadian-style fiberglass canoes had been used a good deal in the Northern Territory. Wildlife officers had often employed them in fieldwork, for bird studies, for locating crocodile nests and for crocodile counts. They were considered as safe as any other small craft. A perception which Val Plumwood was about to change.

On the first day she went out with the canoe she experienced no problems. She felt happy in the craft and confident in handling it. The rangers had told her not to go in the mainstream of the river because the current ran strongly. They recommended she stay in the backwaters and this suited her. The birds were exciting. She took her binoculars, ate lunch on the bank, had a brief walk and returned later in the afternoon. It was a good day.

The second day, February 19, 1985, was quite different. The Northern Territory Wet was running late and the countryside was very dry. Thunder-clouds had been building up in the usual way. But the annual monsoon deluge was well behind schedule.

The day was overcast and fine rain was falling. She had not intended to go out on the river again—her plan had been to go walking. "But I was feeling unwell, so I thought that, after all, I'd use the canoe once more to get to where the birds were. Then I'd have a short walk."

She went down to the landing and launched the canoe about 11 A.M. Almost at once she felt that the atmosphere was quite different to the previous day.

"I was immediately uneasy. I felt that there was something there, that hadn't been around the day before. It's hard to describe—a feeling of unseen menace, I suppose. Whatever it was I felt vulnerable. The canoe seemed very close to the water."

She paddled down river in the backwater, the blade dipping in regular strokes. Trying to talk herself out of the unease.

It was a sort of anabranch joining the main river at both ends. A quiet backwater and normally very pretty. But not that day. "The rain began early and soon became so heavy that I had to keep stopping to empty the canoe. Because of the unease I was very careful not to get out in the water. I always stepped onto land." She stopped again for lunch and went for a short walk in the escarpment country with her binoculars, observing the birds.

"The rain became heavier and heavier until it became an incredible deluge. It was actually the start of the Wet, though I didn't realize it at the time."

The feeling of vulnerability, that she shouldn't be there, persisted. It was particularly strong at one spot on the river. "I could see a particular rock formation some distance away across the East Alligator River—one rock balanced on another. Every time I looked at it I got scared. The other circumstances of the day troubled me. It was a sort of non-specific feeling that something just wasn't right. I shouldn't be there.

"I had no idea why that balancing rock should frighten me and it was irritating. Rational thinkers aren't supposed to be like children afraid of the dark."

However, rationalize as much as she could, she couldn't rid herself of the feeling. An instinct that somewhere there was trouble about.

For that reason she turned the canoe around and set off for home in the rain much earlier than intended. It was about 3:30 P.M. and the rain and squalls of wind were still increasing.

She reached the place in the waterway, a bend, where she had experienced particular uneasiness earlier. Later an old crocodile shooter told her that the crocodile would have been watching her and that she was probably subconsciously aware of the presence.

The crocodile would have awaited her return.

As she paddled back that way something caught her eye. "I noticed a piece of driftwood and thought to myself, 'That wasn't there earlier.' . . ."

In a short time she realized that the "driftwood" was a crocodile ("I saw its yellow eyes") and that she was going to pass quite close to it.

"At that point I hadn't connected my uneasiness with crocodiles. The popular notion was that you wouldn't be attacked in boats. So when I saw it I thought, 'That's all right. A crocodile. How interesting' . . ."

Nonetheless she paddled intending to go wide of the crocodile, not wishing to pass too close to it. It was a discourtesy to intrude on wild animals. Besides—now she saw those eyes—there was the start of a shiver up her spine.

But whatever she did with the paddle she seemed to be on a collision course. At the time she thought that the current—now running faster because of the rising water—was carrying her toward it. It did not occur to her that the crocodile was deliberately intercepting her. Events began to occur quickly.

Canoe and crocodile converged. "There was a tremendous bang on the side of the canoe. I didn't know whether the crocodile was lashing out with its tail or banging with its head. I was too petrified to look.

"For a moment I froze. I thought, 'No. This isn't happening. Not to me. They don't attack boats!' "

But the crocodile was real, it was there and it was unquestionably hostile. "It kept bashing at the canoe. One part of my mind kept asking, 'Why?—Why me?' The other part was trying to be practical, trying to decide what to do."

"The problem was that it was all so unexpected. Obviously I had to make a split-second decision. Over to the right was a shallow, wide sandbank which I would have had to wade across. On the other side was a steep muddy bank, two to three meters high, and growing out of the water a couple of big paperbarks with low, spreading branches. It seemed a great idea to go over there and climb up into the tree. The rain didn't help. It was still pouring down."

BANG! BANG!

The crocodile kept hitting the canoe. Plainly something had to be done and at once. She paddled for the bank, mind in a whirl; the rain still came down hard.

"They said later that the crocodile might have been being

territorial and had mistaken the canoe for another crocodile which had to be driven out of its area. But crocodiles see well, I understand, and the canoe looks nothing at all like another crocodile. Also the canoe was bigger, so if that was the reason it was a pretty brave crocodile. But looking back, I recall that it was looking at me and I think that was the crux of it."

Val Plumwood paddled hard, trying not to panic. When she reached the paperbarks the crocodile was still alongside. Those yellow eyes blazing up at her.

She stood up in the canoe. The crocodile looked even more interested. "Go away!" she yelled, waving her arms as though it were a naughty child, or a disobedient dog. Trying to bluff and hide her fear.

"We had a minute or so of staring into each other's eyes. I was trembling with fear, absolutely terrified. Yet there was still a part of me that couldn't believe it was real. This couldn't be happening to me. . . ."

The crocodile seemed to be tensing, humping its back. "I had the feeling it was getting ready to do something. So I jumped for the tree. There were three or four branches like steps and I pictured myself climbing up them to safety."

She jumped and reached the first branch, seeking to push herself up higher into the tree. But in the same moment the crocodile also leaped. Faster by far than her. It was a lightning upward thrust out of the water that was quicker than the human eye. The typical crocodilian strike which anticipates the movement of the prey.

There was an instant of shock and horror as it surged up and grabbed her with a crash of jaws between the legs. "It was unbelievably fast. I had sort of stepped up with one leg and it came up in a blur from below like a giant pair of spiked pincers. Before I could move or react it had grabbed me at the top of its jump. As it fell back it just tore me out of the tree by throwing its body into a roll.

"Once it got hold of me I had no chance at all. I couldn't believe the strength. The sheer power was enormous."

The crocodile took her down underwater into a series of death rolls, seeking to disorient her, to exhaust her and then hold her down and drown her.

"Gee, that roll! I'd never experienced anything remotely like it. I was helpless against that kind of strength. The river was a kind of black, watery pit and I was being thrashed around like some rag doll in a berserk washing machine. At the time there wasn't a lot of pain. But because of where it had grabbed me, up between the legs, I thought I was going to lose my sexual organs.

One tooth, in fact, had gone in beside the vagina and back as deep as the coccyx—about four inches. That kind of worry may have seemed irrational—after all I knew I was going to die. But I didn't want to be mutilated. Just terror, terror, terror . . ."

The washing machine motion stopped. The jerking, tearing, threshing rolls. The crocodile was holding her down now, to drown her.

With astonishment, Val Plumwood realized that her head was just high enough for her to catch a breath at the surface. She had water in her lungs. She was choking, breathing half water, but now she could at least get air. Sweet, pure, wonderful air. It tasted so good.

If the water had been deeper, if the rolling had lasted another minute, she would probably have drowned. "But the crocodile had a bad grip on the lower part of my body and the water was too shallow, only up to my chest. With an effort I was able to get my head up and breathe.

"There were two sets of rolls, then a distinct gap between, as though the crocodile was getting its own breath back. When it rolled me it seemed like eternity.

"I expected it to roll me again. To keep on doing it and force my head underwater. I thought every breath would be my last so I sucked in as deep and hard as I could. I was just astonished that with that strength it didn't do exactly what it wanted with me. There seemed nothing I could do to stop it."

But there was. As she choked and gasped and struggled for breath she saw within reach one of the overhanging branches of a freshwater mangrove. "It was just so lucky!" She grabbed it as hard and strong as only a drowning person can.

Disconcerted, the crocodile let go. It had used a good deal of its own strength in the attack and in the rolling, and the prey was still vigorously alive.

It would try for a better grip.

As it opened its jaws Val Plumwood dragged herself toward the mangrove by her grip on the root. "And sort of dodged around behind the tree. . . ."

But where next? In her confusion Val repeated her earlier mistakes. Awkwardly, fumbling, blood running down her legs below her torn shorts, she dragged herself up into the tree again.

It seemed like one of those nightmares where things keep repeating themselves. Once more the crocodile leaped from the water. The blur of movement, the flash of spiked teeth, the physical impact and the crash of jaws across her body— this time the upper left thigh.

As it dragged her out of the tree again back down into the river she felt pure despair, her breath choked off by the splash as they struck the water together. Predator and prey.

Again the rolls, disorientation. "I thought I'd rather go through anything but one more of those rolls. There wasn't a lot of pain. But there was a hot feeling in my thigh. I knew the teeth had gone in deep. It all seemed so wasteful. I thought, 'I'm going to die and no one will ever know what happened. How I've suffered. They'll think I've just drowned!' The crocodile was growling in its throat—it seemed terribly angry. I was just so terrified. An agony of terror—I thought, 'Please no—don't let it roll me again!' But it did. A third time.

"By this time I was weaker. It would have been impossible to feel any more fear. But I was despairing. It seemed so futile, so stupid to die like that, without a reason. I tried to feel back along its head—thinking of jabbing my fingers in the crocodile's eyes. I found two sort of leathery sockets. I had a sort of debate with myself as to whether I would make it angrier or not if I attacked it. Then I decided to try a jab. But there was no response and I realized I had my fingers in its nostrils.

"By the end of the third roll I thought I'd really had it. I was thinking 'I wish to God it would finish me off quickly. I don't want to die so slowly and unpleasantly.' Then my waving arms touched the tree branch again—almost as though I was reliving the first effort—and I grabbed it with whatever strength I had left. I knew I couldn't last through any more rolls."

"Then, astonishingly, when it seemed to be all over—The End—it released me again. I guess it was to change grip, maybe to try to get me higher up the body so it could hold me under. But once again I managed to dodge around the tree. This time I didn't make the mistake of trying to climb up into the branches."

"I flung myself up the bank. But it was steep slippery mud. Twice I just slithered back. That was the real nightmare—picturing the crocodile waiting for me at the bottom to grab me again."

"The third time I found that if I stuck my fingers into the mud I could claw myself up inches at a time. I had no idea where the crocodile was—whether it was a few inches behind me, or still back in the water. I didn't dare look around. I was concentrating all my efforts on dragging myself up that slippery bank."

"But I reached the top—to my utter, utter amazement, because I never expected to get away—and I stood up and set off on a sort of hysterical flopping half-crawl, half-run, trying to put distance between me and the river. I knew immediately I was hurt but I didn't dare pause or look back."

"So I flopped along not being able to run fast because my left leg wouldn't work properly and I actually thought it (the crocodile) had done something to my knee. I kept thinking 'the bastard's done my knee.' "

"But nothing mattered in the face of the wild elation—an absolute euphoria. I was alive! Against all expectations I was alive! I had got away! It sounds silly now. A crazy, light-headed feeling."

The euphoria did not last long. She was in a serious predicament. Somehow she had to get back to the East Alligator ranger base. It was out of the question to go back and look for the canoe. But without it she had to cross the swamp and some tributary streams. For her now, any water held terror beyond her physical capacity. But water was everywhere.

She was aware that her injuries were serious—she hadn't the courage to take off her shredded shorts to see exactly how bad—but she knew that she could not go long without medical attention. She took off her singlet, then her bra and used them as bandages and a tourniquet. "A big piece of my left thigh was sort of hanging off and flopping about. It was a miracle the bite missed the femoral artery. But it ripped the muscles and tendons. At one time I had wanted to die. But now I wanted to live. The desire, the determination was very strong."

Gritting her teeth she set off. Every step was pain and her left leg simply would not do what she wanted. But the training of those years of walking stood her in good stead. Putting one foot in front of the other. Making distance, even when it hurt. "Concentrate, Val, concentrate! . . ."

Meantime the rain poured down, huge drops, splashing on the leaves. Bouncing in the puddles, washing the blood off her legs. Rivulets spreading across the earth to join up into a continuous shining sheet of water as the monsoon broke. The ground seemed to be moving water. The flood was coming. Squalls of wind tossed the treetops. There was an eerie grey-green light over everything. The end of the world could have come on just such a day.

In her shocked state, stumbling along, Val Plumwood began to be afraid of losing consciousness. She still had on her raincoat and shorts with her familiar compass swinging

around her neck. The temperature was a hothouse 35°C with
steam rising up from the rain. But she felt cold and was shivering from shock and fright, and sick and nauseous. The
numbed and dizzy disorientation of clinical shock after a serious injury.

Minutes seemed hours, as though time was part suspended.

The attack had occurred about 4 P.M. The struggle felt as
though it had lasted an eternity. Now it seemed ages ago.

The events and the abnormal darkness of the day, the rain
sluicing down, all created an atmosphere of impending doom
and her spirits sank correspondingly lower.

"The worst thing was that I knew that I was in a swamp
that was likely to become flooded with such heavy rain. I was
terrified that if I passed out and became unconscious I would
drown and be washed away. No one would ever know what
had happened to me. Strange how important that was. It
seemed so cruel to have survived something as dreadful as the
crocodile and then die out there in the mud."

As daylight faded she began to feel increasingly light-
headed and apprehensive. Twice she had to cross deeper
streams. With great effort, concentrating on each step, she
walked up them until she found overhanging branches she
could hold on to to cross.

She knew she could not get back to the ranger station
across the water on her own and that she would have to rely
on being found. The closer she could get to the swamp the
better chance she had of being found. But she could not expect a search party until the next day and by then she might
be dead. How could she maximize her chances of being
found? How could she survive the coming night?

She was getting very weak and dizzy now and knew she
could not go much farther. Her left leg was a weak, useless,
floppy thing, foreign to her body, except that it burned with
pain. Several times she blacked out momentarily. But she was
dreadfully afraid that if she lay down where she was, no one
would find her. So she staggered and crawled on, to try to

find a better place to lie down for the night, a place where her body could be seen.

"Concentrate, Val! You can do it! You know you can!"

Forcing one foot after the other. Making distance. She tried all the old bushwalking tricks to goad herself along. Each tree passed was a progress. Each bend in the creek an event.

At one stage her paddle passed her floating down the creek. She looked around hopefully for the canoe. But no such luck. She had had too much luck already. Just to get away from those jaws! She looked behind her apprehensively, the horror still upon her.

Now as she walked she began calling out, tears running down her cheeks, imploring the crocodile to forgive her for intruding in its territory. Apologizing to it, over and over. "I'm sorry. I'm sorry. I shouldn't have come to your place. Just let me go!"

Meantime, as darkness fell at the ranger base, each family was isolated in its own house by the rain pouring down. Rain hammering on the roofs, splashing on the patios, a deluge. It was no night to be outside. Everyone was indoors.

Val Plumwood could have died in the swamp that night. She was quite right in her fear that no one would have known what happened. By morning the whole area was under water. The paddle washed far, far down the river.

But one man noticed that there was no light in her caravan. Rangers are more conscious about these things than other people. The darkened van troubled Greg Miles. He knew that she had been out in the canoe on the previous day and the canoe was normally kept down at the mooring. He supposed that he could at least go down and check that it was there. The darkened caravan nagged at him. When he knocked there was no response. There was nobody there. Where could she be on a night like this? She should have been back hours before. . . . Miles started the three-wheeler bike and steered out into the slush. The road was a running muddy river, though the rain had temporarily eased.

At the mooring the rain had stopped. But now his eyes narrowed in concern. The canoe was definitely missing. If Val Plumwood had gone out in it she should have been back in the afternoon. It was now well after dark. He consulted his watch. It was 8 o'clock. He peered out into the darkness. The night was now still.

Val Plumwood had reached the edge of the swamp. For the last part of the distance she crawled. "Concentrate, Val, concentrate. Don't give up!"

Dragging herself through the mud and sticks. "Concentrate. . . ." But still a sheet of water divided her from the ranger base. She could go no farther. She settled down on a spot and lay down to await the coming night. Her chances of survival seemed remote.

As darkness fell, she hoped for unconsciousness but it did not come and the line between recognizable and tortured fantasy became blurred. It was not surprising. After what had happened, and as a normal reaction of shock to the injury, she had become part delirious.

She became convinced that the crocodile was somewhere around. Worse still, as she lay there in her pain she heard splashings. It was no imagination. There were crocodiles in her area. She also heard dingoes howling close by. "They had different, distinctive voices. I thought there were about six of them. I knew they wouldn't hurt a healthy person. But what about someone wounded, weak and bleeding? Someone unconscious on the ground? . . ."

Then she saw a light and heard a distant sound of a motor. It came bobbing through the darkness and stopped. She was vaguely aware that the rain had stopped and the wind quietened into what seemed an unnatural hush. She raised herself on her elbow and called with all her strength across the dark swamp, "Help!" again and again. "Help!"

Greg Miles thought he heard a sound. A cry? . . . A despairing human cry? He cocked his head and listened. Yes, there it was again. A long way away. But unmistakably a human voice. "Stay there. We're coming back to get you!" he called across the black water.

Confronted with an emergency the Australian National Parks and Wildlife Service rangers are a well-trained body of men. Greg Miles could have no knowledge of what had happened to Val Plumwood, of course. But he recognized an emergency. For anyone to be out in the darkness, crying out, something serious must have happened. At any rate she needed help and quickly, by the sound of it.

He started the bike, spun it around and roared off to raise the alarm. To put into practice the accustomed emergency routine of organizing the ranger boat and the other people to help in an immediate search.

Val Plumwood could not understand why the light went away. It seemed so cruel to see that faint flicker of hope disappear. But then nothing seemed to make much sense any more.

Had the voice—whoever it was—heard her call? Would they come to find her?

Despair. As she lay in the rain, hordes of mosquitoes—happy for the Wet—buzzed around tormenting her. "The whining was dreadful and they bit and bit. There was nothing I could do."

At last, at last the boat. The sounds of lights and voices. She was too weak even to sit up. Thank God there was still a lull.

"Help!"

"Help!"

"Help! Oh, God help me!"

"I shouted for all I was worth. Just lying on the ground, too weak to sit up or do anything else . . ."

But they heard her. An hour earlier in the downpour, with the wind roaring in the trees, she would have had no chance.

Even so it took them some time to locate the injured, terrified woman, lying among the trees. But eventually the spotlight, filtering through trunks, lighted on her. It paused, then returned and held her in its beam.

Rescue!

"I was never so pleased to see anyone. I greeted them with an enormous smile, despite my injuries. I was so glad, so glad to see human faces. They were so capable, so comforting."

The rangers in their turn were shocked when they saw her injuries and heard her story, garbled and incoherent.

Val Plumwood recalls little of that time. She had used all her determination and reserves of strength to reach the perimeters of safety. Now she let go—pain and consciousness together came and went in waves. But she does recall hearing two of the four rangers in the boat talking matter-of-factly about shooting the crocodile. She was horrified. "I really asked them in the strongest possible terms, in fact begged them, not to do it. It seemed so unfair." It wasn't the crocodile's fault, she said. She had been the intruder. . . . It was the crocodile's territory.

Greg Miles and the other Australian National Parks and Wildlife rangers found her five hours after the attack. The following day Darwin newspapers carried an account of her ordeal and the 13-hour, all-night drama involved in getting her to hospital in Darwin after the boat rescue in the swamp.

"DARWIN: Val Plumwood, from Braidwood in the NSW southern tableland, was admitted to Royal Darwin Hospital about 8 A.M. yesterday after an all-night rescue operation to get her out of the floodbound Kakadu National Park to an ambulance for the 200-kilometer journey to Darwin after being attacked by a 4.5-meter saltwater crocodile.

"In teeming rain she was transported in three separate cars and three boats across potholed bush roads and through swamps before reaching the ambulance (at the South Alligator River crossing).

"She is understood to be in a serious but stable condition after undergoing surgery for deep gashes in her buttocks and legs."

Greg Miles was quoted:

"She was not a pretty picture. She was very desperate and there was a lot of blood. She had the horrific experience of having to assess her own wounds but she was still able to smile."

"She is an extremely courageous woman to have survived the terror of the attack in the first instance, and then to tourniquet those horrible wounds and then try to get help."

Val Plumwood remained seriously ill in the hospital for some time. As a complication to her major injuries she contracted a pseudomonas infection, either from the swamp mud or from the crocodile's teeth, which caused her doctors grave concern and which also could have killed her. It was the third time her life had been at risk. She survived the infection as she had the other ordeals. After a long month in Darwin she was transferred to Sydney's Royal North Shore Hospital for skin grafts and further surgery over another month.

For a time she feared she might never walk normally again. But skillful surgery and her own determination saw a remarkable recovery. Nonetheless there were some permanent effects from the injuries.

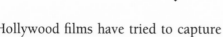

Hollywood films have tried to capture the terror of what Val Plumwood experienced, but they never have and never will. Surely, if we could harness the courage she showed, clawing up that muddy bank, tending her own wounds, forging on and refusing to give up, we might change the world. No less miraculous than her survival was her resiliency. Many such victims have survived only as gutted wrecks, never willing or able to integrate the shock and resume anything but shadow lives. The glory here is that Plumwood pushed through the horror and outrage of the attack and rejoined the living, and did so without wanting to convert every Australian crocodile into a pair of loafers. Believe this: many bitter survivors of animal attacks dedicate the rest of their lives to evening the score with the shark or the crocodile or the big cat. After the attack, Plumwood wrote: "Humans tend to think that whenever there's a conflict with an animal like a crocodile, the crocodile has to be eliminated. I think it's unfair. The world is not just a place for human beings. It's a crocodile world too. That goes for other less-than-popular (with humans) creatures like snakes. I can't see why people can't live with crocodiles in Queensland. They do in the Territory. It's mainly a matter of modifying expectations."

But how do you change your expectations? Obviously, you don't swim in a river teaming with crocodiles. In most places where crocs and humans are likely to cross paths, warnings are everywhere, if not on signs, then on the lips of every local. If you ignore the warnings and get bitten by a crocodile in a nonswimming area, who is to blame? But blame is a slippery word here. There is always risk when entering crocodile country. Know that crocs will attack anything they believe is edible. And, as this story shows, these "big daddies" are quicker than lightning. Like hippos, crocs stay close to the water, so at least we know where they should be.

J.L.

---◆---

The Spotted Devil of Gummalapur

Kenneth Douglas Stuart Anderson

The leopard is common to practically all tropical jungles, and unlike the tiger, indigenous to the forests of India; for whereas it has been established that the tiger is a comparatively recent newcomer from regions in the colder north, records and remains have shown that the leopard—or panther, as it is better known in India—has lived in the peninsula from earliest times.

Because of its smaller size and decidedly lesser strength, together with its innate fear of mankind, the panther is often treated with some derision, sometimes coupled with truly astonishing carelessness, two factors that have resulted in the maulings and deaths of otherwise intrepid but cautious tiger hunters. Even when attacking a human being the panther rarely kills, but confines itself to a series of quick bites and quicker raking scratches with its small but sharp claws; on the other hand, few persons live to tell that they have been attacked by a tiger.

This general rule has one fearful exception, however, and that is the panther that has turned man-eater. Although examples of such animals are comparatively rare, when they do occur they depict the panther as an engine of destruction surpassing his far larger cousin, the tiger. Because of his smaller size he can conceal himself in places impossible to a tiger, his need for water is far less, and in veritable demoniac cunning and daring, coupled with the uncanny sense of self-preservation and stealthy disappearance when danger threatens, he has no equal.

Such an animal was the man-eating leopard of Gummalapur. This leopard had established a record of some forty-two human killings and a reputation for veritable cunning that almost exceeded human intelligence. Some fearful stories of diabolical craftiness had been attributed to him, but certain it was that the panther was held in awe throughout an area of some 250 square miles over which it held undisputable sway.

Before sundown the door of each hut in every one of the villages within this area was fastened shut, some being reinforced by piles of boxes or large stones kept for the purpose. Not until the sun was well up in the heavens next morning did the timid inhabitants venture to expose themselves. This state of affairs rapidly told on the sanitary condition of the houses, the majority of which were not equipped with latrines of any sort, the adjacent waste land being used for the purpose.

Finding that its human meals were increasingly difficult to obtain, the panther became correspondingly bolder, and in two instances burrowed its way in through the thatched walls of the smaller huts, dragging its screaming victim out the same way, while the whole village lay awake, trembling behind closed doors, listening to the shrieks of the victim as he was carried away. In one case the panther, frustrated from burrowing its way in through the walls, which had been boarded up with rough planks, resorted to the novel method of entering through the thatched roof. In this instance it found itself unable to carry its prey back through the hole it had made, so in a paroxysm of fury had killed all four inhabitants of the hut—a man, his wife and two children—before clawing its way back to the darkness outside and to safety.

Only during the day did the villagers enjoy any respite. Even then they moved about in large, armed groups, but so far no instance had occurred of the leopard attacking in daylight, although it had been very frequently seen at dawn within the precincts of a village.

Such was the position when I arrived at Gummalapur, in response to an invitation from Jepson, the District Magistrate, to rid his area of this scourge. Preliminary conversation with some of the inhabitants revealed that they appeared dejected beyond hope, and with true Eastern fatalism had decided to resign themselves to the fact that this shaitan, from whom they believed deliverance to be impossible, had come to stay, till each one of them had been devoured or had fled the district as the only alternative.

It was soon apparent that I would get little or no cooperation from the villagers, many of whom openly stated that if they dared to assist me the shaitan would come to hear of it and would hasten their end. Indeed, they spoke in whispers as if afraid that loud talking would be overheard by the panther, who would single them out for revenge.

That night, I sat in a chair in the midst of the village, with my back to the only house that possessed a twelve-foot wall, having taken the precaution to cover the roof with a deep layer of thorns and brambles, in case I should be attacked from behind by the leopard leaping down on me. It was a moonless night, but the clear sky promised to provide sufficient illumination from its myriad stars to enable me to see the panther should it approach.

The evening, at six o'clock, found the inhabitants behind locked doors, while I sat alone on my chair, with my rifle across my lap, loaded and cocked, a flask of hot tea nearby, a blanket, a water bottle, some biscuits, a torch at hand, and of course my pipe, tobacco and matches as my only consolation during the long vigil till daylight returned.

With the going down of the sun a period of acute anxiety began, for the stars were as yet not brilliant enough to light the scene even dimly. Moreover, immediately to westward of the village lay two abrupt hills which hastened the dusky uncertainty that might otherwise have been lessened by some reflection from the recently set sun.

I gripped my rifle and stared around me, my eyes darting in all directions and from end to end of the deserted village street. At that moment I would have welcomed the jungle, where by their cries of alarm I could rely on the animals and birds to warn me of the approach of the panther. Here all was deathly silent, and the whole village might have been entirely deserted, for not a sound escaped from the many inhabitants whom I knew lay listening behind closed doors, and listening for the scream that would herald my death and another victim for the panther.

Time passed, and one by one the stars became visible, till by 7:15 P.M. they shed a sufficiently diffused glow to enable me to see along the whole village street, although somewhat indistinctly. My confidence returned, and I began to think of some way to draw the leopard toward me, should he be in the vicinity. I forced myself to cough loudly at intervals and then began to talk to myself, hoping that my voice would be heard by the panther and bring him to me quickly.

I do not know if any of my readers have ever tried talking to themselves loudly for any reason, whether to attract a man-eating leopard or not. I suppose there must be a few, for I realize what reputation the man who talks to himself acquires. I am sure I acquired that reputation with the villagers, who from behind their closed doors listened to me that night as I talked to myself. But believe me, it is no easy task to talk loudly to yourself for hours on end, while watching intently for the stealthy approach of a killer.

By 9 P.M. I got tired of it, and considered taking a walk

around the streets of the village. After some deliberation I did this, still talking to myself as I moved cautiously up one lane and down the next, frequently glancing back over my shoulder. I soon realized, however, that I was exposing myself to extreme danger, as the panther might pounce on me from any corner, from behind any pile of garbage, or from the rooftops of any of the huts. Ceasing my talking abruptly, I returned to my chair, thankful to get back alive.

Time dragged by very slowly and monotonously, the hours seeming to pass on leaden wheels. Midnight came and I found myself feeling cold, due to a sharp breeze that had set in from the direction of the adjacent forest, which began beyond the two hillocks. I drew the blanket closely around me, while consuming tobacco far in excess of what was good for me. By 2 A.M. I found I was growing sleepy. Hot tea and some biscuits, followed by icy water from the bottle dashed into my face, and a quick raising and lowering of my body from the chair half a dozen times, revived me a little, and I fell to talking to myself again, as a means of keeping awake thereafter.

At 3:30 A.M. came an event which caused me untold discomfort for the next two hours. With the sharp wind banks of heavy cloud were carried along, and these soon covered the heavens and obscured the stars, making the darkness intense, and it would have been quite impossible to see the panther a yard away. I had undoubtedly placed myself in an awkward position, and entirely at the mercy of the beast should it choose to attack me now. I fell to flashing my torch every half minute from end to end of the street, a proceeding which was very necessary if I hoped to remain alive with the panther anywhere near, although I felt I was ruining my chances of shooting the beast, as the bright torchbeams would probably scare it away. Still, there was the possibility that it might not be frightened by the light, and that I might be able to see it and bring off a lucky shot, a circumstance that did not materialize, as morning found me still shining the torch after a night-long and futile vigil.

I snatched a few hours' sleep and at noon fell to questioning the villagers again. Having found me still alive that morning—quite obviously contrary to their expectations—and possibly crediting me with the power to communicate with spirits because they had heard me walking around their village talking, they were considerably more communicative and gave me a few more particulars about the beast. Apparently the leopard wandered about its domain a great deal, killing erratically and at places widely distant from one another, and as I had already found out, never in succession at the same village. As no human had been killed at Gummalapur within the past three weeks, it seemed that there was much to be said in favor of staying where I was, rather than moving around, in a haphazard fashion, hoping to come up with the panther. Another factor against wandering about was that this beast was rarely visible in the daytime, and there was therefore practically no chance of my meeting it, as might have been the case with a man-eating tiger. It was reported that the animal had been wounded in its right forefoot, since it had the habit of placing the pad sideward, a fact which I was later able to confirm when I actually came across the tracks of the animal.

After lunch, I conceived a fresh plan for that night, which would certainly save me from the great personal discomforts I had experienced the night before. This was to leave a door of one of the huts ajar, and to rig up inside it a very lifelike dummy of a human being; meanwhile, I would remain in a corner of the same hut behind a barricade of boxes. This would provide an opportunity to slay the beast as he became visible in the partially-opened doorway, or even as he attacked the dummy, while I myself would be comparatively safe and warm behind my barricade.

I explained the plan to the villagers, who, to my surprise, entered into it with some enthusiasm. A hut was placed at my disposal immediately next to that through the roof of which the leopard had once entered and killed the four inmates. A very lifelike dummy was rigged up, made of straw, an old pillow, a jacket, and a saree. This was placed within the doorway of the hut in a sitting position, the door itself being kept half open. I sat myself behind a low parapet of boxes, placed diagonally across the opposite end of the small hut, the floor of which measured about twelve feet by ten feet. At this short range, I was confident of accounting for the panther as soon as it made itself visible in the doorway. Furthermore, should it attempt to enter by the roof, or through the thatched walls, I would have ample time to deal with it. To make matters even more realistic, I instructed the inhabitants of both the adjacent huts, especially the women folk, to endeavor to talk in low tones as far into the night as was possible, in order to attract the killer to that vicinity.

An objection was immediately raised, that the leopard might be led to enter one of their huts, instead of attacking the dummy in the doorway of the hut in which I was sitting. This fear was only overcome by promising to come to their aid should they hear the animal attempting an entry. The signal was to be a normal call for help, with which experience had shown the panther to be perfectly familiar, and of which he took no notice. This plan also assured me that the inhabitants would themselves keep awake and continue their low conversation in snatches, in accordance with my instructions.

Everything was in position by 6 P.M., at which time all doors in the village were secured, except that of the hut where I sat. The usual uncertain dusk was followed by bright starlight that threw the open doorway and the crouched figure of the draped dummy into clear relief. Now and again I could hear the low hum of conversation from the two neighboring huts.

The hours dragged by in dreadful monotony. Suddenly the silence was disturbed by a rustle in the thatched roof which brought me to full alertness. But it was only a rat, which scampered across and then dropped with a thud to the floor nearby, from where it ran along the tops of the boxes before me, becoming clearly visible as it passed across the comparatively light patch of the open doorway. As the early hours of the morning approached, I noticed that the conversation from my neighbors died down and finally ceased, showing that they had fallen asleep, regardless of man-eating panther, or anything else that might threaten them.

I kept awake, occasionally smoking my pipe, or sipping hot tea from the flask, but nothing happened beyond the noises made by the tireless rats, which chased each other about and around the room, and even across me, till daylight finally dawned, and I lay back to fall asleep after another tiring vigil.

The following night, for want of a better plan, and feeling that sooner or later the man-eater would appear, I decided to repeat the performance with the dummy, and I met with an adventure which will remain indelibly impressed on my memory till my dying day.

I was in position again by six o'clock, and the first plan of the night was but a repetition of the night before. The usual noise of scurrying rats, broken now and again by the low-voiced speakers in the neighboring huts, were the only sounds to mar the stillness of the night. Shortly after 1 A.M. a sharp wind sprang up, and I could hear the breeze rustling through the thatched roof. This rapidly increased in strength, till it was blowing quite a gale. The rectangular patch of light from the partly open doorway practically disappeared as the sky became overcast with storm clouds, and soon the steady rhythmic patter of raindrops, which increased to a regular downpour, made me feel that the leopard, who like all his family are not over-fond of water, would not venture out on this stormy night, and that I would draw a blank once more.

By now the murmuring voices from the neighboring huts had ceased or become inaudible, drowned in the swish of the rain. I strained my eyes to see the scarcely perceptible doorway, while the crouched figure of the dummy could not be seen at all, and while I looked I evidently fell asleep, tired out by my vigil of the two previous nights.

How long I slept I cannot tell, but it must have been for some considerable time. I awoke abruptly with a start, and a feeling that all was not well. The ordinary person in awaking takes some time to collect his faculties, but my jungle training and long years spent in dangerous places enabled me to remember where I was and in what circumstances, as soon as I awoke.

The rain had ceased and the sky had cleared a little, for the oblong patch of open doorway was more visible now, with the crouched figure of the dummy seated at its base. Then, as I watched, a strange thing happened. The dummy seemed to move, and as I looked more intently it suddenly disappeared to the accompaniment of a snarling growl. I realized that the panther had come, seen the crouched figure of the dummy in the doorway, which it had mistaken for a human being, and then proceeded to stalk it, creeping in at the opening on its belly, and so low to the ground that its form had not been outlined in the faint light as I had hoped. The growl I had heard was at the panther's realization that the thing it had attacked was not human after all.

Switching on my torch and springing to my feet, I hurdled the barricade of boxes and sprang to the open doorway, to dash outside and almost trip over the dummy which lay across my path. I shone the beam of torchlight in both directions, but nothing could be seen. Hoping that the panther might still be lurking nearby and shining my torchbeam into every corner, I walked slowly down the village street, cautiously negotiated the bend at its end, and walked back up the next street, in fear and trembling of a sudden attack. But although the light lit up every corner, every rooftop and every likely hiding place in the street, there was no sign of my enemy anywhere. Then only did I realize the true significance of the reputation this animal had acquired of possessing diabolical cunning. Just as my own sixth sense had wakened me from sleep at a time of danger, a similar sixth sense had warned the leopard that here was no ordinary human being, but one that was bent upon its destruction. Perhaps it was the bright beam of torchlight that had unnerved it at the last moment; but whatever the cause, the man-eater had silently, completely and effectively disappeared, for although I searched for it through all the streets of Gummalapur that night, it had vanished as mysteriously as it had come.

Disappointment, and annoyance with myself at having fallen asleep, were overcome with a grim determination to bag this beast at any cost.

Next morning the tracks of the leopard were clearly visible at the spot it had entered the village and crossed a muddy drain, where for the first time I saw the pugmarks of the slayer and the peculiar indentation of its right forefoot, the paw of which was not visible as a pugmark, but remained a blur, due to this animal's habit of placing it on edge. Thus it was clear to me that the panther had at some time received an injury to its foot, which had turned it into a man-eater. Later I was able to view the injured foot for myself, and I was probably wrong in my deductions as to the cause of its man-eating propensities; for I came to learn that the animal had acquired the habit of eating the corpses that the people of that area, after a cholera epidemic within the last year, had by custom carried into the forest and left to the vultures. These easily procured meals had given the panther a taste for human flesh, and the injury to its foot, which made normal hunting and swift movement difficult, had been the concluding factor in turning it into that worst of all menaces to an Indian village— a man-eating panther.

I also realized that, granting the panther was equipped with an almost-human power of deduction, it would not appear in Gummalapur again for a long time after the fright I had given it the night before in following it with my torchlight. It was therefore obvious that I would have to change my scene of operations, and so, after considerable thought, I decided to move on to the village of Devarabetta, diagonally across an intervening range of forest hills, and some eighteen miles away, where the panther had already secured five victims, though it had not been visited for a month.

Therefore, I set out before 11 A.M. that very day, after an early lunch. The going was difficult, as the path led across two hills. Along the valley that lay between them ran a small jungle stream, and beside it I noted the fresh pugs of a big male tiger that had followed the watercourse for some two hundred yards before crossing to the other side. It had evidently passed early that morning, as was apparent from the minute trickles of moisture that had seeped into the pug-marks through the river sand, but had not had time to evaporate in the morning sun. Holding steadfastly to the job in hand, however, I did not follow the tiger and arrived at Devarabetta just after 5 P.M.

The inhabitants were preparing to shut themselves into their huts when I appeared, and scarcely had the time nor inclination to talk to me. However, I gathered that they agreed that a visit from the man-eater was likely any day, for a full month had elapsed since his last visit and he had never been known to stay away for so long.

Time being short, I hastily looked around for the hut with the highest wall, before which I seated myself as on my first night at Gummalapur, having hastily arranged some dried thorny bushes across its roof as protection against attack from my rear and above. These thorns had been brought from the hedge of a field bordering the village itself, and I had had to escort the men who carried them with my rifle, so afraid they were of the man-eater's early appearance.

Devarabetta was a far smaller village than Gummalapur, and situated much closer to the forest, a fact which I welcomed for the reason that I would be able to obtain information as to the movements of carnivora by the warning notes that the beasts and birds of the jungle would utter, provided I was within hearing.

The night fell with surprising rapidity, though this time a thin sickle of new moon was showing in the sky. The occasional call of a roosting jungle cock, and the plaintive call of peafowl answering one another from the nearby forest, told me that all was still well. And then it was night, the faint starlight rendering hardly visible, and as if in a dream, the tortuously winding and filthy lane that formed the main street of Devarabetta. At 8:30 P.M. a sambar hind belled from the forest, following her original short note with a series of warning cries in steady succession. Undoubtedly a beast of prey was afoot and had been seen by the watchful deer, who was telling the other junglefolk to look out for their lives. Was it the panther or one of the larger carnivora? Time alone would tell, but at least I had been warned.

The hind ceased her belling, and some fifteen minutes later, from the direction in which she had first sounded her alarm, I heard the low moan of a tiger, to be repeated twice in succession, before all became silent again. It was not a mating call that I had heard, but the call of the King of the Jungle in his normal search for food, reminding the inhabitants of the forest that their master was on the move in search of prey, and that one of them must die that night to appease his voracious appetite.

Time passed, and then down the lane I caught sight of some movement. Raising my cocked rifle, I covered the object, which slowly approached me, walking in the middle of the street. Was this the panther after all, and would it walk this openly, and in the middle of the lane, without any attempt at concealment? It was now about thirty yards away and still it came on boldly, without any attempt to take cover or to creep along the edges of objects in the usual manner of a leopard when stalking its prey. Moreover, it seemed a frail and slender animal, as I could see it fairly clearly now. Twenty yards and I pressed the button of my torch, which this night I had clamped to my rifle.

As the powerful beam threw across the intervening space it lighted a village cur, commonly known to us in India as a "pariah" dog. Starving and lonely, it had sought out human company; it stared blankly into the bright beam of light, feebly wagging a skinny tail in unmistakable signs of friendliness.

Welcoming a companion, if only a lonely cur, I switched off the light and called it to my side by a series of flicks of thumb and finger. It approached cringingly, still wagging its ridiculous tail. I fed it some biscuits and a sandwich, and in the dull light of the starlit sky its eyes looked back at me in dumb gratitude for the little food I had given it, perhaps the first to enter its stomach for the past two days. Then it curled up at my feet and fell asleep.

Time passed and midnight came. A great horned owl hooted dismally from the edge of the forest, its prolonged mysterious cry of *"Whooo-whooo"* seeming to sound a death knell, or a precursor to that haunting part of the night when the souls of those not at rest return to the scenes of their earthly activities, to live over and over again the deeds that bind them to the earth.

One o'clock, two, and then three o'clock passed in dragging monotony, while I strained my tired and aching eyes and ears for movement or sound. Fortunately it had remained a cloudless night and visibility was comparatively good by the radiance of the myriad stars that spangled the heavens, a sight unseen in any of our dusty towns or cities.

And then, abruptly, the alarmed cry of a plover, or "Did-you-do-it" bird, as it is known in India, sounded from the nearby muddy bank on the immediate outskirts of the village. *"Did-you-do-it, Did-you-do-it, Did-you-do-it, Did-you-do-it,"* it called in rapid regularity. No doubt the bird was excited and had been disturbed, or it had seen something. The cur at my feet stirred, raised its head, then sank down again, as if without a care in the world.

The minutes passed, and then suddenly the dog snapped fully awake. Its ears, that had been drooping in dejection, were standing on end, it trembled violently against my legs, while a low prolonged growl came from its throat. I noticed that it was looking down the lane that led into the village from the vicinity of the bank.

I stared intently in that direction. For a long time I could see nothing, and then it seemed that a shadow moved at a corner of a building some distance away and on the same side of the lane. I focused my eyes on this spot, and after a few seconds again noticed a furtive movement, but this time a little closer.

Placing my left thumb on the switch that would actuate the torch, I waited in the breathless silence. A few minutes passed, five or ten at the most, and then I saw an elongated body spring swiftly and noiselessly onto the roof of a hut some twenty yards away. As it happened, all the huts adjoined each other at this spot, and I guessed the panther had decided to walk along the roofs of these adjoining huts and spring upon me from the rear, rather than continue stalking me in full view.

I got to my feet quickly and placed my back against the wall. In this position the eave of the roof above my head passed over me and on to the road where I had been sitting, for about eighteen inches. The rifle I kept ready, finger on trigger, with my left thumb on the torch switch, pressed to my side and pointing upward.

A few seconds later I heard a faint rustling as the leopard endeavored to negotiate the thorns that I had taken the precaution of placing on the roof. He evidently failed in this, for there was silence again. Now I had no means of knowing where he was.

The next fifteen minutes passed in terrible anxiety, with me glancing in all directions in the attempt to locate the leopard before he sprang, while thanking Providence that the night remained clear. And then the cur, that had been restless and whining at my feet, shot out into the middle of the street, faced the corner of the hut against that I was sheltering and began to bark lustily.

This warning saved my life, for within five seconds the

panther charged around the corner and sprang at me. I had just to press the torch switch and fire from my hip, full into the blazing eyes that showed above the wide-opened, snarling mouth. The .405 bullet struck squarely, but the impetus of the charge carried the animal on to me. I jumped nimbly to one side, and as the panther crashed against the wall of the hut, emptied two more rounds from the magazine into the deadly, spotted body.

It collapsed and was still, except for the spasmodic jerking of the still-opened jaws and long, extended tail. And then my friend the cur, staunch in faithfulness to his newfound master, rushed in and fixed his feeble teeth in the throat of the dead monster.

And so passed the "Spotted Devil of Gummalapur," a panther of whose malignant craftiness I had never heard the like before and hope never to have to meet again.

When skinning the animal the next morning, I found that the injury to the right paw had not been caused, as I had surmised, by a previous bullet wound, but by two porcupine quills that had penetrated between the toes within an inch of each other and then broken off short. This must have happened quite a while before, as a gristly formation between the bones inside the foot had covered the quills. No doubt it had hurt the animal to place his paw on the ground in the normal way, and he had acquired the habit of walking on its edge.

I took the cur home, washed and fed it, and named it "Nipper." Nipper has been with me many years since then, and never have I had reason to regret giving him the few biscuits and sandwich that won his staunch little heart, and caused him to repay that small debt within a couple of hours, by saving my life.

———◆———

Is it possible to paint a more terrifying tableau of terror and hopelessness than that suffered by the villagers of Gummalapur, people trembling in their rickety shanties behind tin doors secured by flimsy boxes or piled stones? Picture yourself, moon-eyed, all senses on alert, as a man-eating panther lurks outside on the meager thatch of your roof, snarling, rooting, and perhaps burrowing in and dragging you, your spouse, or a screaming child off into the darkness. Your neighbors sit petrified and powerless. And if you should live through the night, you're too frightened to leave your shack except as part of an armed party, twenty strong. Caligula never dominated people as entirely as did the spotted devil of Gummalapur. After reading this story, it's easy to understand how the panther took on the devil's aspect and how Anderson would be hailed as a living god when he did the devil to death. In the context of this story, we can appreciate the legendary status granted the bygone white hunter. But when all is said and done, we can't forget that Kenneth Douglas Stuart Anderson would have been a very dead legend had it not been for a stray dog, then and always man's best friend.

J.L.

The Deadly Leopard

Peter Hathaway Capstick

He was still alive when the men reached my camp on the Munyamadzi River, although I'm sure I don't know why. It was *emeni,* or "midday," in Zambia's dry season, when everything was sensibly quiet in the heat, including me, propped in the cool shade of the sausage tree grove with a sweating Lion Lager in my fist. Things had been thankfully slow in the mayhem department for the last few days, and my game-control duties of shooting raiding elephant or chasing poachers had been light. But there was always the paperwork in quintuplicate, and I had spent the past three days filling in "kill" forms and making the usual inventory of ivory, confiscated poached trophies, and such ready for the official vehicle that would be by any time to pick them up. The three scouts under my command were afield on duty with their bicycles and not due back until the day after tomorrow, leaving in camp only me, old Silent, and a kitchen *toto* to fetch water and wood.

Silent saw them first. Five hundred yards away, walking across a flat, were two Awiza tribesmen carrying a blanket-wrapped form slung from a pole between them. My guts told me what would be in that dirty, torn blanket. It looked as if the vacation was over. When they laid it down and unwrapped the tattered edges, even I, who can happily eat my lunch seated on the rapidly rotting carcass of a dead elephant, had to force down a gag. The poor bugger looked as if he'd spent a weekend in a blender set at "cole slaw." Except for the burning, unblinking eyes that stared at me, I would have thought the best medicine for him was a shovel. But he was not only alive, he talked!

The bush African seems to defy most of the rules of modern medicine. You can convince him that he's been hexed, and he'll lie down and die on you in about four days. Yet I've seen him ripped from crotch to clavicle by rhino horn and double-tusked through the intestines by elephant, burned, infected, and shredded by lion, and within a few weeks he's back on his feet again, scarred but healthy despite wounds that would have sickened a Spanish Inquisitor.

As it happened, despite the fact that quite a lot of his face was hanging free from its moorings, he looked vaguely familiar. When he spoke, I realized that I knew him from the village, for he called me by my African name, Nyalubwe. *Nyalubwe* means "leopard" in Chenyanja, which seemed to throw a macabre humor over the situation. It developed that it had been my namesake that had replatted the man, whose name was Chisi. Silent brought the big medicine kit and had the kitchen lad set water to boiling. We lifted him to the makeshift dining table and, as I listened to him tell his tale, I did what I could to reassemble the jigsaw puzzle of torn flesh.

It had been about an hour after dawn, the sun still low behind the yellow thorn trees, when Chisi had walked from the village with his son, a six-year-old named Ntani, to check his snares for *khwali*, or partridge. Although I of course did not permit the setting of wire snares for game in my area and treated offenders firmly in the extreme, I didn't see much harm in the snaring of an odd francolin or guinea fowl for the family pot, provided only grass cord or light bark fiber was used. At the edge of a grassy *vlei,* dead in the winter dryness, they entered the cover with Chisi leading and carrying his spear. The boy followed close behind.

As I poured disinfectant into one fang hole in his arm and watched it run out another, he went on, his voice oddly calm and clear despite the obvious pain he must have been in since the shock had worn off. At the third snare they visited, a cock guinea fowl was struggling mightily and broke the anchor line just as the pair came up, dashing off still half-tied into the bush. Chisi watched, amused, as the boy chased it through the cover, which was very thick. Then came a shriek cut short, a thrashing, then silence. As quickly as he could run, Chisi bulled through the grass, his spear drawn back for a throw. As he pounded along he almost ran over the grisly scene: a big male leopard standing over his son, whose neck was still in the cat's jaws. So fast that it was a blur, the leopard dropped the child and instantly sprang at Chisi, who managed to thrust at it with the spear blade, missing the chest but cutting deeply into the stomach.

The leopard's lightning charge knocked Chisi down backward, and the cat fastened its long teeth into his arm. The deadly hind legs windmilled, seeking and finding his belly and thighs, flashing claws shredding meat to the bone. A forepaw hooked and held for a moment in the flesh of the right side of his face, pulling the tissue into red ribbons as the claws tore free.

I had just finished stuffing the odd loops of Chisi's guts back into his lower chest and hopefully taping on a sterile, wet compression pack when he finished his story. He had lain for some time, stunned, staring at the lifeless body of his son a few feet away. Already the flies were gathering. Fortunately, the two men who had carried Chisi to my camp had noticed the vultures gathering and gone to investigate, finding him and the boy. They had rigged the *machila* with the blanket and stopped by the village on their way to send a party for Ntani's body.

It was the middle of the afternoon before I had done what I could for Chisi, closing the worst tears with butterfly tape sutures instead of sewing him up, for almost surely infection would develop later. With a butt full of penicillin and a dreamy smile on his face from the injection of morphine, he calmly watched me radio for a Game Department car to pick him up and take him to a small dispensary about fifty miles away that had an Indian doctor. I would have taken him myself, but I had business back in that high grass.

Silent and I, guided by the two Awizas, whose names I don't recall, arrived at the *vlei* at half-past four in the afternoon, having left Chisi in the care of the kitchen helper until the Land Rover arrived. I'd done all I could and now the most important matter was to settle accounts with the *nyalubwe* before tragedy struck again. Man-eating leopards are more rare than lions or crocs with a taste for human flesh, although they often are killers of opportunity, taking a child or woman just as they would any other primate such as a baboon or monkey. Still, from Chisi's account, I think that the leopard merely happened to be in the grass and heard the excited cries of the guinea fowl. As it raced on a collision course with Ntani to catch the bird, the cat probably grabbed the child by reflex as the better meal. Of course, this was mere theory, but as there had been no reports of man-eating leopards in this district for more than a year, I guessed that this was the case. No matter. The cat was wounded and would still chew and claw the hell out of anybody who crossed him and might even turn full man-eater if incapacitated and unable to take his normal smaller prey. Among other things, that's what I got paid to prevent.

I killed the hunting car's engine two hundred yards from the place indicated by the two men and stepped out, Silent hopping out the rear with my "possible" bag mentioned elsewhere. That there may be no speculation, I am the worst sort of sissy, bearing an ingrained aversion to having my throat torn out, my face pulled off (as happened to old friend Heinz

Pullon), or my insides hooked outside by wounded leopards. In anticipation of such hazards, I also keep a few items handy that are sort of alternative contents to the "possible" bag. I think of it as my Black Knight outfit. Not that you'd want to fight the Battle of Hastings in it, but there's a lot of good reasons to insulate yourself as best you can from things that bite. The primary feature is a leather jacket to which I spent a day riveting big slabs of Formica in a flexible pattern. The second item is an antique U.S. Marine leather neck guard originally designed to protect the throat and neck from sword cuts. Not that I don't trust the Marine suppliers of yore, but just to be extra safe, I riveted it over with sheet metal. Somehow, it gives me the appearance of wearing stainless steel dentures. I used to have my old football helmet, too, but some tribesman stole it one dark evening and it is no longer in inventory.

Silent checks out the bag's contents, and you shrug into the jacket, finally lacing up the neck protector. No need for the old .375 H&H; this will be a very personal affair. The Winchester Model 12 slides, silver-worn and sharp with the odor of WD-40, from the soft case. You thumb six rounds into the unplugged magazine, jack one into the chamber, and top off the cargo with a seventh in the magazine. You try not to notice the deep claw marks on the pump's forestock, for they tend to bring up disconcerting memories of similar situations. Unable to think of even the most improbable excuse to stay around the car puttering with your gear, you reluctantly head for the *vlei* and all that bloody grass, feeling much like a gladiator waiting for the main gate to the arena to open. You have decided not to take Silent (who is now pouting) because it's just too thick, and you may have to snapshoot in any direction in a fraction of a second. He would not look very good after a charge of buckshot from a couple of feet and, anyway, good gun-bearers are getting hard to find.

The first fifty yards take a full half-hour. The gun is held well back on the hip to prevent the leopard from getting between you and the muzzle. The worn walnut is slippery with sweat. Each step is taken with infinite slowness on the out-side edges of the feet. Visibility is down to eight or ten feet, so there's no point in looking for the leopard himself. Instead, you watch for the movement of grass he will be forced to make when he charges. Oh, he'll charge all right, because he's almost certainly still here, lying up and licking his wounds. You follow the trail of Chisi and his son, which blends with the in-and-out bloodstained route of the other men and the party recovering the child's body, until you finally reach the unmistakable place of death. There are large gouts of arterial blood, which means that Ntani bled to death instead of dying of a broken neck. A few feet away there is another patch of torn and red-smeared ground where Chisi was mauled. From the spoor leading away into the grass, it would seem that Chisi may have "washed his spear" well in the leopard, hope-fully well enough that he'll be nice and dead, although you somehow doubt it. Well, at least you have something going for you with a blood trail to follow and enough time gone by for the cat's wounds to slow him down. Whoa. Wait a minute. You know better than that. Expect the worse and there'll be no big surprises.

The sun is starting to slip away by the time you find the soggy place in the grass thirty yards from the mauling where the leopard stopped to lie up for a while. Not good. He's moved and you sure don't need shadows on top of everything else. But he's still trickling a thin, crimson spoor on the stalks, so you had better get in gear before you lose the light.

Step. Turn completely around. Listen. Listen hard for the tiniest swish of grass. You've got to know where he's coming from before you can put up that defensive thunderstorm of lead. Twenty more yards. And then you know.

Everything has slowed down except your heart. As if by hypnosis, your eyes are drawn to the grass at your right front. Was there a sound so faint that you didn't consciously regis-ter it? Hard as you stare, nothing of the leopard is to be seen. But you're somehow positive he's there, off to the right of the

blood spoor, waiting for you on his own track. You can actually feel his eyes through the stems and stalks. Slowly, the
shotgun swivels to cover the spot, which looks exactly like
every other khaki clump of growth. Sweat is pouring down
your face despite the fact that you feel oddly cool. What next?

You don't have to decide. He does. Like an uncoiling steel
spring, he's in the air, launched directly at your face, his mask
a twisted, befanged horror framed between extended, inward-
turned paws that are studded with long, hooked, white claws.
Despite his speed, you somehow have time to notice every de-
tail of his awful, sinuous, lithe beauty. Then the Winchester
fires—a short, hard bark—and his left front paw disintegrates
as the solid charge of shot shreds it on the way to his neck
and head. With the trigger still held back, you instantly work
the pump. The second swarm of buckshot pours into him as
the firing pin slams the primer on the return stroke. A hole the
size of your clenched fist appears just where his throat meets
his upper chest, visibly slowing him in flight with the terrible
impact of the charge. He turns in the air as if somersaulting to
crash on his back, as limp as a plastic bag of sausage meat,
landing a yard short of your feet with a soggy thump. Without
any hesitation, you kill him again. It's a shame to blow such a
hole in that beautiful amber and anthracite skin, but you
know his will be more easily repaired than your own. Lordie,
but a cigarette will taste good with a long swig from the water
bag.

You give a sharp whistle and hear Silent fire up the old
hunting car as you slip out of the armored jacket and untie
the neck protector. In a few minutes, guided by your whistles,
the grass is folding down and the hood of the Rover pokes its
way into view with the snout of a prehistoric, metal hippo.
You go through the usual, highly flattering version of what
happened for his sake so that he may enjoy the status of having a *bwana* worth lying about. The leopard is easily loaded
onto an old piece of canvas and swung over the edge of the
pickup tailgate when you happen to notice that your bush

shorts are really quite soggy. Must have spilled some water from the jawsack. Yeah.

Capstick once wrote

> It's my personal belief, based on experiences I would much rather not have had, that there is no circumstance so potentially lethal in taking any of the "Big Five" (lion, leopard, elephant, rhino, and cape buffalo) as following up a wounded but still active leopard. Because of their size, the big boys—elephant, rhino, and buff—can usually be spotted in time to kill or turn a charge. Even the lion, although he's more likely to kill you if he is close enough, will betray a charge with a growl or roar, giving you some idea where he's coming from. Not the leopard. He never gives you an edge, saving that rush or spring for such close quarters that he's sure he will nail you or he won't come. With the most perfect camouflage in nature, he's invisible until he turns into a golden-dappled streak of pure malevolence, biting and clawing with such speed that cases have been recorded in which wounded leopards have mauled as many as seven armed men in a single rush and then melted back into the grass before anyone could do anything but bleed.

As other stories in this collection assure us, Capstick has not embroidered the "pure malevolence" of a wounded leopard. So why would the man strap on that jury-rigged black knight getup and track the blood spoor of the deadliest creature on four legs? Machismo? Psychologists define that as "strength without truth." And what of the various maxims that one should face a tough duty with a stiff upper lip; the more dangerous the task, the greater the chance for "self-improvement?" In light of Capstick tracking that beast, the business of a stiff upper lip and the swindle about self-improvement seem perfect examples of machismo: they contain no emotional truth at all. Maxims, at best, are good only to help suppress fear. Here, raw fear is the truth. What, then, are the genuine reasons that drew Capstick into the hedge to face a leopard?

Few things are harder to determine than what motivates people to face danger deliberately. I'm reminded of Oscar Hammerstein's words: "Who can explain it, who can tell you why? Fools give you reasons; wise men never try." He has a point. A few insightful people, however, have commented on the subject; a particularly elegant one was Italian mountaineer Giuseppe Gervesutti, who said: "A person never feels so alive as when he walks in the shadow of his own doom. The glory of life itself can be fully appreciated only after we've come within a hair's breadth of losing it."

A sense of duty, a stiff upper lip, a chance to improve oneself. Perhaps these did play a part in getting Capstick's feet moving toward the dire hedge and the wounded cat, but only Gervesutti gives us glimpse of *why* Peter Hathaway Capstick chose his line of work in the first place.

J.L.

Savaged by a Lion

Ben East

The leopard bait was an impala that had been shot and hung in an acacia tree on the edge of a dry river bed. It had ripened in the hot sun for three days, long enough that John Kingsley-Heath and Bud Lindus were sure if there were leopards in the country they could not resist it. The hunting party had hung a number of baits—zebra, gazelle, impala—but for some reason both the hunter and his client felt that this was the one that would get them what they hoped for.

The time was August of 1961. Kingsley-Heath was on safari with the Lindus family—Bud, his wife Pamela and their fourteen-year-old son Roger—along the Ruaha River in the semi-arid desert country of central Tanganyika.

Operating out of Nairobi and conducting hunts in Kenya and Tanganyika at the time, John Kingsley-Heath was rated among the top hunters of Africa. He had held a professional hunter's license since 1951, barring a brief interruption during the Mau Mau insurgency, and was known by name and reputation to many sportsman in the United States.

Lindus was a retired oil salesman from Honolulu and he

and his wife were old clients of John's. Bud rated African hunting very high, and Pam and the boy shared his enthusiasm for it.

The chief object of their hunt was a trophy lion. Two years earlier Lindus and Kingsley-Heath had been led up the garden by an enormous maned male, in the Kajiado district of Kenya. That one had the uncanny ability of disappearing at exactly the crucial minute, whether they approached him on foot or by car. He hid in the day, ate their baits at night. Try as he would, Bud never locked his sights on him.

He had come back to Africa now determined to do better. Buffalo and kudu also were on his list, he wanted a good leopard for his wife, and if they came across an elephant with satisfactory ivory they didn't mean to turn it down.

They had sharpened their hunting senses on buffalo in the thick bush country of northern Tanganyika before moving down to the Ruaha. Two bulls had gotten within a yard of them before going down permanently. After that they felt they were ready to take on most anything, including the biggest lion in Tanganyika—if they could find him.

Camp had been made on the bank of the Ruaha, under large acacia trees that spread overhead like huge green umbrellas. Thousands of sand grouse watered in front of the tents every morning. The wing shooting was superb, and they were soon out of shotgun shells and sending back to Nairobi for more.

Alvin Adams, a friend of Bud's from the States, had come out to join them for a fortnight, wanting a big leopard, and was hunting with Kevin Torrens, the second hunter/guide on the safari. The numerous leopard baits had been hung partly in the hope of helping Al get his cat.

Bud and John hunted lions, elephants and kudu for days with no success. Tracks and signs were plentiful but they couldn't come across anything of the sort they desired. Leopards refused to touch their baits, and they began to wonder whether their luck was in or out. But when they hung the impala in the tree at the edge of the river two or three miles from camp, Kingsley-Heath had a hunch they were going to get action.

Three days later, Bud, Pam, Roger and Kingsley-Heath came into camp for a late lunch. When they finished their sandwiches and tea, John suggested they go have a look at the bait. It was time for things to be happening if they were going to.

They drove out in the hunting car, through dry scrub-thorn country, taking along two gunbearers and trackers, Kiebe and Ndaka. Halfway to the leopard bait, however, John sent them off to follow up some elephant tracks, with instructions to rejoin him near the bait tree.

They drove the hunting car to within six hundred yards of the tree, left it and walked carefully the rest of the way. One peep around a large bush told them that a leopard had taken his fill. It was late afternoon, almost time for him to return for his evening meal. There was not a minute to waste. They'd sit for him at once.

It was quickly decided that Pam should have the first chance. Bud and Roger went back to the car to wait; Pam and John stole carefully up behind a thick bush and secreted themselves in the bottom of it, first making a little hole for their guns.

Pam was carrying a rifle of European make, as light as the Tanganyika game laws permitted, for the sake of minimum recoil, mounted with a 4X scope. Kingsley-Heath's gun was a Winchester Model 70 in .300 Magnum caliber, with a 6X Kollmorgen scope. Neither of the rifles was right for what was going to happen, but there were good reasons for choosing them.

Sitting up for a leopard can be sticky business, especially if you are not used to it, since you know that if you fail to make a clean kill you have one of the most dangerous animals in

Africa to deal with. Pam was nervous, and said so. Unless the cat fell dead at her shot, she had asked John to back her by putting another into it immediately.

That was why the hunter had brought the scope-sighted Winchester. A 6-power scope may seem unusual for a job of that kind, but it has its advantages. To begin with, it enables the hunter to increase his distance from the bait, and often he can select a better hide by moving off a bit. Too, a leopard almost invariably comes on a bait late, when the light is failing fast, and the more powerful the scope the better its light-gathering ability.

Had the two gunbearers not been off following the elephant tracks, Kingsley-Heath would have had one of them in the hide with him, carrying his .470 Westley-Richards double, but he couldn't very well handle two guns by himself.

He and Pam made themselves comfortable, with their rifles trained on the spot where they expected the leopard to appear. For twenty minutes nothing happened. The silence of late afternoon was settling over the bush. Puffs of wind blew through the acacias, stirring up little dust devils, but the breeze was from the bait tree, so they had no worry on that score. Now and then a bird twittered, and the shrunken river whispered around its sandbars. Except for those small sounds nothing broke the stillness.

It was an uneasy quiet, and as the minutes dragged on John grew suspicious. Was the leopard approaching from behind? Had he scented them and slunk away? They keep a sharp watch all around, nothing stirred in the brush or grass. The time ticked off and John's uneasiness grew. Then, suddenly aware of movement or noise behind his right shoulder, he turned his head ever so slowly as was looking a huge maned lion in the face, just twenty feet away.

The situation was clear to him in a flash. The leopard had not come to the bait because the lion had kept him away. The lion couldn't reach the impala himself, and now, hungry, disappointed and angry, he had spotted the two people in their thick bush, had not seen or smelled enough of them to know what they were, and was stalking them for a kill. And he was close enough for that final, lightning-fast rush with which a lion takes his prey at the last second.

When Kingsley-Heath turned his head and they stared into each other's eyes, the big cat recognized him for a man, but it was too late for that to make any difference. John saw his expression change from the intent look of a stalking lion to one of rage. His face wrinkled in a snarl and he bunched his feet under him for the spring.

It all happened a great deal quicker than it can be told. One second John was staring at the leopard bait. The next he was looking the lion in the face, the animal was gathering for its leap, and the hunter was swiveling his rifle around from the hip.

"The eyes of the big cats, I think more than those of any other animal, mirror what is going on behind them," Kingsley-Heath told me long afterward. "At the instant of attack those of a lion seem to be on fire. The burning yellow orbs of this big male fairly blaze into mine, and there was no misreading their message."

John did not wait to bring the rifle to his shoulder. He was sitting on his hunkers, as he described it, and he whipped the gun across his knees and pulled off at the lion, all in a split second, trying for the thickness of the shoulder. The shot struck a little too far back, but the animal reacted to the 180-grain softnose as most lions do to a hit, whipping his great head around and biting savagely at the wound.

Pam and John were not conscious, then or afterward, of running through the six-foot bush where they were hidden, but they did it and never got scratched. They got clear and raced for the car. In the thicket behind them simba was growling and roaring and thrashing in pain and anger. They ran until they were far enough away to be safe, then stopped to get their breath and congratulate themselves on a very narrow escape.

"We have to get this chap," John told Bud when they finished panting out their story. "You and I will have a lion war."

The two gunbearers were not yet back from their elephant scout. Pam and Roger were left in the car, and Lindus and Kingsley-Heath took their heavy rifles and hurried off. John's was the .470, Bud's a .450/400 double made by Manton & Co., a London firm. Both were good lion guns, but because they had not expected to encounter a lion and had thought they might get a chance at an elephant that afternoon instead, they had only solid ammunition along instead of the softnose loads they would have preferred.

The lion had left the place where he was shot, and it was plain from the blood that he was reasonably well hit. The blood spoor led down to the bottom of the dry river bed. There, although he was bleeding heavily, it had dried in the sand and lost its color, making it difficult to follow in the evening light.

He ran along for a ways under the bank, climbed up a small gully and went into the thicket of mswaki bush, and evergreen that grows like very thick weeping willow, with the outer branches draping down to the ground, leaving a cave-like opening underneath. This thicket was leafy, the lion had left little signs on the hard-baked sand, and the two men went down on their hands and knees to track him through gaps between the bushes.

They didn't crawl far before Kingsley-Heath pulled up short. "This is no good," he told Bud. "If we go ahead with our eyes on the ground we'll walk right down his throat. Kiebe and Ndaka should be back at the car by now. We'll get them and let them do the tracking while we watch over their heads.

Kiebe was a particularly good man to have along in such a situation. A Kamba by tribe, he had hunted for twenty-five years, eight of them with John, and before that with Miles Turner, one of the most famous of East African white hunters. John had saved Kiebe's life a time or two, and the tracker had saved his. Tracking down a wounded lion was nothing new to Kiebe, and he was absolutely fearless. Kingsley-Heath knew he could count on him no matter what happened. The second tracker, Ndaka, was a standin, but willing and brave.

The two of them were at the car, and the four hurried back to the place where John and Lindus had left the lion track. It was lucky they had quit when they did, for fifteen yards ahead they found the bloodstained bed where he had been lying.

He had moved about thirty yards into another thicket while they were gone, still bleeding. They tracked him foot by foot, with Kiebe in the lead. It was not a job any of them liked, but they had no choice. Once a hunter starts an affair of that kind it's up to him to finish it, no matter how sticky it gets.

Kiebe wiped warm blood off the leaves, and held up a hand to warn his bwana that they were getting close. Then the lion announced his presence with an angry growl from the mswaki just ahead, and they saw him race across a narrow opening into the next brush.

It was almost dark now and in a very few minutes they'd have to give up. They left the track and circled, hoping to push him into the open, but nothing stirred and no sound came from the thicket. They wasted precious time, the light got worse, and at last John whispered to Kiebe in Swahili, "This is for tomorrow. We'll let him stiffen up and beat him out in the morning."

The tracker's reply was a finger jabbed sharply to the left. There, under a low bush fifty feet away, the lion lay broadside, breathing heavily, watching them. John could barely make out the shape of his heavy body in the dusk.

The range was close enough, but they were shooting with open sights in very bad light and had to be absolutely certain of a hit. Kingsley-Heath took Lindus by the arm without saying a word, and they shortened the distance to forty feet, moving warily to the nearest tree, where a leaning branch would give them a rest for the rifles.   ✗

The shot belonged to the client, and since Bud was a first-class rifleman John did not expect there'd be any need for him to fire. But he made one serious mistake. He overlooked the fact that in the half-darkness the flash of Bud's rifle would blind him for the critical fraction of a second when the lion might come for them in case Bud failed to kill it where it lay.

Bud's 400-grain solid took the cat in the shoulder a bit high, but because the bullet was not a softnose it went all the way through without opening up, doing only slight damage to the lungs. And in that instant when John should have hammered another in, he could see neither lion, thicket nor anything else.

In all the years he had been a professional hunter, and all the hunting he had done on his own, Kingsley-Heath had been attacked by an animal only once. That had happened in the very beginning, when he was training under an old hunter. He approached too close to an elephant he was stalking, and the bull knew he was there. It waited until he was within reach, grabbed him up in its trunk and sent him flying into a swamp tangle. By good fortune he escaped unhurt except for a slight stiffness in the right shoulder. This time he wasn't going to be that lucky.

The lion came in a rush the first few feet, then covered the rest of the distance in two great bounds. John had time only to yell at Bud to dodge behind him, when a huge ball of snarling fury landed at his feet.

He slammed a 500-grain solid into the great cat's head between the eyes, point blank, and but for a fluke that would have ended the affair. But because the lion was badly wounded, when he hit the ground in front of John his head jerked forward and down, like a man who has jumped off a stool. The heavy bullet struck him square between the eyes, as the hole in the skull showed later, but instead of going through his brain and leaving him deader than mutton, it passed down between his lower jaw bones and out at the side of his throat, hardly more than blinding him with the rifle flash.

He leaped past John within a foot and landed between the two men, headed for Bud. John saw that Bud's rifle was tangled in branches and he couldn't get it down. The quarters were too close for a second shot without endangering him. Kingsley-Heath took one step and clubbed the lion on the head with the barrels of his .470 as hard as he could. The cat grunted, shook his head and wheeled around, and before John had time to pull the second barrel he pounced.

A quarter ton of growling, raging cat hit Kingsley-Heath full length and he went down as if he had been electrocuted. It felt about like that, too, he said afterward. There was no pain and he was not stunned, but the shock of the blow as the lion crashed into him, with its forepaws over his shoulders and its huge body bearing him to the ground, was beyond description. His gun went flying out of his hands and then he was lying on his back with the lion on top of him, its front legs wrapped around him and its paws under his shoulder blades.

A lion, even wounded, often pauses for a second after his initial leap has knocked his victim down, and this one did just that. That tiny pause saved John Kingsley-Heath's life. He knew that within a second or two the lion would bite him through the head, and he smashed his right fist into its nose with every ounce of strength he had. He broke the bones of the hand, but the lion opened its mouth at the punch, maybe to growl, and John followed through. He rammed his fist down its throat, and its teeth closed on his arm halfway to the elbow.

John heard the bones crunch, but in a strange detached way, not as a sound from outside, but as if he were hearing the arm break from inside his own body.

So long as he kept his fist down its gullet, the lion could

not get at his head or throat. He could feel its claws under him, ripping his sheepskin hunting jacket to shreds and his back with it. He knew that if it got its hind feet in his belly it would tear his guts out with one rake. He twisted on his left side, drew his legs up to protect himself, and concentrated on trying to keep his broken arm in its mouth.

The statement has been made more than once that a man attacked by one of the big carnivores is overcome with a merciful numbness, so that he feels little or no pain or fright at the time, perhaps because shock overwhelms his nervous system. Kingsley-Heath thinks the part about being benumbed is true, but for a different reason. The victim of such an attack is fighting for his life and knows it, and he believes that a man in that situation has little sense of feeling. In his own case he felt very little pain through the whole mauling. When it was all over his back looked as if he had been flogged with a cat-o-nine tails, but it hadn't hurt while it was happening.

Nor did he smell the lion's breath or have any sensation of feeling its mane against his face, although he knew it was there. He did have a bad nightmare in the hospital later, when he felt lion saliva all over his fingers and woke up in a cold sweat trying to get his mangled arm out of the cat's jaws.

Actually the lion took care of that for him. It shook him as a terrier shakes a rat, rolling him back and forth, and freed itself of his fist and arm about the way a big fish gets rid of a bait.

It takes far longer to describe such an experience than to live through it. Everything was happening at once. "Get my gun!" John yelled at Kiebe in Swahili. "Kamata bunduki yanga! Piga the bloody thing!" Piga means hit, but in this case he meant shoot and the tracker knew it.

Then he saw Bud come into sight over the lion's rear quarters and the .450 bellowed twice. But because John was lying under the cat Bud could only shoot far back. They learned later that he broke a hind leg but the lion paid no attention, neither flinching nor turning its head. It just went on growling and mauling its victim, and took no notice of Bud, Kiebe or Ndaka. That is typical lion behavior. Once simba gets his victim down he stays with it. A wounded leopard will rush from one member of a party to another, biting at the first man he can reach, then striking instantly at a fresh victim, only to leave that one and run for the next. A lion takes time to finish what he begins.

Kiebe grabbed up Kingsley-Heath's gun now, checked swiftly to see which barrel was loaded, ran in and shoved the muzzle against the lion's shoulder, heedless of his own danger. But from where John lay beneath the brute he saw that the bullet, whatever it might do to the cat, would also smash through his knees, and he screamed at Kiebe, "For God's sake don't shoot there!"

The tracker backed away a step and blasted the one round remaining in the .470 into the lion's back just behind the shoulders. That put Kiebe out of the fight, for the rest of John's ammunition was in his pocket under the lion. But the shot was strong medicine and well placed. It broke the spine, and the beast twisted off him. A wounded lion doesn't quit as long as he is breathing, however, and this one wasn't finished yet. Back it came on its front legs, with its back end dragging, and quick as John moved he wasn't quick enough to get to his feet before it was on him again.

It would have taken him through the left side of the chest with its huge canine teeth, and one bite there meant certain death, but he threw up his left arm to fend it off. He had not time to jam the arm down its throat, as he had done with the right. He simply shoved it into the lion's face. It grabbed and crushed the arm just above the wrist, and once more John heard his own bones break like match sticks, not as he would have heard another man's but as a noise coming from inside him.

At this point Ndaka did a very brave thing. He threw himself on the lion and stabbed it again and again in the ribs and throat with a 6-inch knife. Then Lindus, who had been stuffing fresh shells into the breech of his double while Kiebe got in his shot, stepped close and sent two more solids crashing into the lion. The great body jerked and sagged and rolled off Kingsley-Heath.

As he struggled to his knees, half helpless from two broken arms, he jabbed his left foot into its face to kick it away. That was the wrong thing to do, even with a lion breathing its last. Its jaws closed on John's shoe and it bit down, and for the third time he heard the crunch of breaking bones, in his foot and ankle now. And that time, he remembered, it hurt like hell! He wrenched his foot free, but the lion died with his shoe in its mouth.

They left the cat where he lay. They'd have to run the risk of hyenas tearing him up before morning. Bud and the natives carried John to the car and wrapped him in the rain curtains to keep him warm. Then they set off in the darkness for camp. There was no moon and they couldn't follow their tire tracks, so rather than get lost they stopped and made a fire, and let off a shot every ten minutes. It's a rule on safari that if anyone fails to return to camp by an hour after dark the search and rescue operation gets under way at once. They knew that by now Kevin Torrens, the other white hunter, was out looking for them.

Kingsley-Heath's wounds had clotted well and he was bleeding only a little, but he drank water like a mad thing. Kiebe and Ndaka left to try to find the way to camp, and shortly after that the injured hunter and his clients heard the hum of a motor, and then the lights of Kevin's Landrover appeared.

It was 2 in the morning by the time they found their way back through the scrub thorn to camp. Torrens cleaned up John's wounds, poured disinfectant into them, and had him swallow three times the normal dose of antibiotic tablets, washing them down with hot tea. Next John got down two cups of soup and began to feel quite comfortable. But about that time he went into shock, started to tremble violently from head to foot and kept it up for hours.

They had a radio telephone in camp, but by now it was Sunday morning (the lion attack had occurred on Saturday evening) and the government radio in Nairobi was closed down, so Torrens left for the nearest phone at Dodoma, a hundred and twenty miles away, thirty of it rough track through the bush, to call for a plane. They had scratched out a small airstrip near camp earlier.

Kevin got through to Peter Whitehead, a manger of a leading Nairobi safari firm, at 6:15 on Sunday morning and forty-five minutes later Dr. Brian McShane, Kingsley-Heath's physician and good friend, was airborne and on the way with a supply of blood and the other things he needed to fix the injured man up temporarily. Bill Ryan, another professional hunter from Nairobi and also an old friend of John's, came along to take over the safari. It was a two-and-a-half-hour flight. They touched down at the camp at 9:30 that morning.

By that time John had sent the safari boys out and they had brought the lion to camp. The hyenas had not molested it, after all. It was a magnificent brute, the biggest Kingsley-Heath had ever had a hand in killing: 10½ feet long and weighing out at 497 pounds. It must have weighed a bit above 500 alive, before it lost blood. There in the Dodoma district the lions live mostly on buffalo and the full-grown males are among the finest trophies in all of Africa. This one was paler than average, but not quite a blond, with a lavish mane. As his friends remarked later, at least John had been savaged by a decent lion, not one with just a ruff around its neck. Bud got the pelt, and it's a safe bet he will never take a trophy that will give him a more exciting time. John kept a tooth and claw and had them mounted as paperweights.

Dr. McShane poured blood into him and set about patching him up for the flight back to Nairobi. He had two broken arms, a broken hand, a foot chewed and badly crushed, a horribly lacerated back and a few deep holes in various parts of his body. As he was being carried into his tent after the attack, he had heard Kiebe tell the other safari boys, "Bwana ameliwas na simba," which is Swahili for, the bwana was eaten by a lion.

Kingsley-Heath entered the Princess Elizabeth hospital in Nairobi that afternoon, August 13, and stayed until October 2. He was on the dangerous list for a few days, but the surgeons repaired his broken bones and by great good fortune he escaped infection, which is very likely to follow an attack by one of the big cats because of their habit of feeding on putrid meat. The fact that he had been able to get down a massive dose of antibiotics a few hours after the accident probably saved his life. He did not think that the lion was cleaner than average.

The mauling proved worse than the aftermath, and most of his stay in the hospital was not a torturous ordeal. He was well enough to leave on an easy safari the day he got out of the hospital.

For the courage he had shown, Kiebe received the Queen's Commendation for Brave Conduct a few months later. Asked what his thoughts were at the time, he replied matter-of-factly, "Do you suppose I am going to do nothing when a lion is about to kill my friend?" And the only reward he wanted was corrugated iron to roof his house.

There was an interesting sequel to the story. On August 12, 1962, a year to the day from the time the lion mauled him, he sat up for leopard at that same tree and at the same hour. He had a lady client again, and they sat in the same bush where Pam and he had waited. The leopard put in an appearance as the light was starting to fade, the client fired and the cat tumbled, hit hard but not dead. In the twinkling of an eye John found himself in exactly the same predicament he had faced on that fateful evening a year earlier, except that this time he was dealing with a leopard rather than a lion. Not that that is much to be preferred.

It was too dark for tracking, so they went back to camp and returned the next morning. The blood spoor led into a bush nearby, and to the hunter's great relief the leopard lay dead there. So if there was any jinx connected with that tree it had been laid to rest. But in all of Africa there is not another tree that John Kingsley-Heath will remember so vividly and long as that acacia on the edge of the dry river bed. He says so himself.

———◆———

For me, the telling lines in this story are when, following their narrow escape after wounding the lion, John Kingsley-Heath turns to his client and says, "We have to get this chap . . . or you and I will have a lion war." So runs the hunter's code: if you wound a predator, you must finish it off no matter the personal danger involved. This code developed because a wound greatly diminishes the beast's ability to hunt, and the animal is then far more likely to drop down the food chain a step or two and go after easier, possibly human, prey. In effect, by wounding the lion, Kingsley-Heath created a potential man-eater. The "huge-maned lion" with the "burning yellow orbs that seemed to fairly blaze into mine" had to be killed. Inherent in the hunter's code is the understanding that hunting predators is risky; likewise, it is reckless and inexcusable to play the game if others must feel the teeth of a wounded lion that a hunter didn't bother to finish off. It's the essence of accountability: the party who starts the ruckus is honor-bound to resolve it, and others should not be made to bear the consequences of a game they never agreed to play.

J.L.

---◆---

Night Attack

Joyce Thompson with Larry Kaniut

Dying was the farthest thing from my mind in September 1972, when my husband Al Thompson and I planned our backpacking trip for trophy moose into the Kenai National Moose Range on Alaska's famed Kenai Peninsula, an area mostly closed to aircraft or tracked vehicles. We planned to catch the last ten days of moose season, which closed the end of September. Al was archery hunting; but if time ran out and he failed to get one, I would shoot one with my rifle.

The night before leaving, we gathered our gear together into one spot, double checking and eliminating any items we could get along without. Al was taking his 65-pound bow and glass arrows tipped with razor sharp, black diamond delta heads. He would carry his .44 Magnum revolver, and I would take my 30.06 rifle. We finished by stuffing our gear into two very full packs.

We adjusted our packs and started down the trail on a typically beautiful Alaskan fall day—the leaves were golden, it was warm and sunny, and the smell of Alaskan autumn filled the air.

Eight and a half bone-weary hours later we reached the area where we wanted to camp. Every muscle in my body ached and my feet were sore. As it was almost dark, we made a hurried camp, fixed something to eat and turned in for the night.

The next day we developed our camp into a very comfortable one. We built a lean-to out of logs and clear plastic, placing boughs on the ground for a mattress and covering them with a plastic floor. The front of the lean-to had a plastic flap to close out the cold night air. Al built a makeshift table from a piece of wood we found. We gathered an abundant supply of firewood and picked up paper and litter left behind by others.

On the third day, before crawling into his bag, Al located matches, a light, placed his .44 Magnum on a piece of yellow paper towel for easier spotting and laid my 30.06 by his side with the safety off and a shell in the chamber. Unlike me, he left his sleeping bag partially unzipped for quick access to a weapon. The combination of a warm sleeping bag, a tired body, and the crackling of the fire soon had me drifting off to sleep.

I was awakened about 4:00 A.M. by Al's whispering into my ear. He had sensed something and whispered to me not to move as something might be out there in camp. I listened, straining to hear a sound which might locate an animal. As I kept watching into the moonlight night, I saw the silhouette of a brown bear move alongside of me.

Al did not see the bear from his position. The animal was only inches from me, with just the plastic between us, and it didn't make a sound. It seemed to be moving away, when all of a sudden the bear was on top of me. He plunged through the top of our lean-to with a bellowing roar. This was Al's first sight of the bear.

Al grabbed the rifle; but with the impact of the bear, the rifle flew from his grip. For a fraction of a second the bear appeared confused as the logs broke and the plastic tore. He stood on his hind legs, towering over us. He was enormous, like a huge, gray driftwood log.

There was no time for Al to locate the .44 revolver. He knew the only way to save me was to immediately distract the bear from me to him. He also reasoned that if he turned his head in search of the revolver, the bear might instinctively go for his neck, thus killing both of us. As the bear dropped to all fours, Al grabbed its head with his left hand and slugged him with his right. The bear grabbed Al's left forearm in his jaws and by standing up, pulled Al out of his sleeping bag, tossing him through the air.

He landed at the foot of the lean-to. Like a flash the animal was over him. Its massive claws ripped through Al's right side, almost penetrating the lung. Its teeth raked along Al's skull, gripping the scalp. The bear picked Al up with its mouth and one foreleg and ran on three legs.

With Al dangling by his scalp, the bear stood straight up shaking his head violently as a cat with a mouse. Al's feet never touched the ground. The bear ran a distance of approximately 25 yards, and a large portion of scalp tore loose from Al's head causing the bear to momentarily lose his grip.

While all this was taking place, I rose, realizing the heavy weight of the animal and horrible noise was gone. Al's sleeping bag was lying beside mine, empty. I had not seen Al's struggle with the beast because my head was covered, and I was baffled as to where he and the bear had gone.

I stood up in my sleeping bag, pulled it down and stepped out of it. Searching for a weapon, I saw the .44 revolver lying on the yellow piece of paper towel. The rifle was not in sight. Where was Al? Where was the bear? Even though it was not total darkness, I could not see any movement or forms nor hear any sound. I had a strong feeling of danger and of the bear charging me at any moment.

My first impulse was to run, to get away from the area. My common sense told me my best chance was to stay in this clearing and in camp as the bear would overtake me, and heading to an area of denser cover would only tend to give him a more secure feeling. My next thought was to stick the revolver in my waistband and try to climb a tree. Unlike black bears, brown bears do not climb trees unless they pull themselves up by using the limbs.

I was dressed completely in white, including socks, which must have made me very visible as I moved in the moonlight. The trees were large with no limbs low enough for me to reach. Dismissing any chance of escape, I cried "God, please help us," and braced myself holding the revolver in both hands. I may not kill a charging bear before he got me, but I would not give up my life without a fight.

As Al was being carried by the bear, he thought, "What a hell of a way to die." Then he thought of me, faced with the shock of my having a dead husband, miles from anywhere or anyone, and having to hike out of there alone. He became angry, and a strong will to fight for survival overcame him.

A brown bear is capable of dragging off a full-grown moose. His strong legs and claws can move boulders and huge hunks of earth. A blow from his paws can break the neck of a moose or another bear. No man could come close to matching his strength. Al realized his only chance was to convince the bear he was dead.

When the scalp tore off and the bear momentarily lost his grip, Al fell onto a hump of moss. He grasped the hump with his right arm, holding his face and stomach down to keep from being ripped open, took a deep breath and held perfectly still. The bear cuffed at him, leaving horrible claw marks all along his side and shoulders. He bit into Al's back twice, while standing over him looking for a sign of life. There was none. Al's playing dead displayed remarkable self-discipline, as the pain was excruciating.

Then I heard the bear. He was moving away from me, heading toward cover in the direction of the little lake in the area. As I stood listening, trying to locate him, I heard Al call to me. He was running toward me. Moving closer to him, I could see his knit shirt was torn and he was covered with blood. "I'm hurt bad, but I'm going to live," he said. In the next breath he ordered, "Find the rifle, quick!"

"Where do you think it is?" I asked.

"Look at the end of the lean-to; it may have landed there," he replied. As he wiped the blood from his eyes, he held the revolver while I searched for the rifle. I had to feel around for it in the darkness. I found it and also a shirt for him to hold on his head, as blood was pouring down over his eyes.

Our minds were working fast, lining out immediate things to do. A fire! Got to get a fire going! Thanks to the dry wood, kindling and paper we had collected on our cleanup this was quickly accomplished. In a few seconds the flames were high.

Al slumped on the sleeping bag. He was cold and started to shake. The temperature was about 25 degrees. He must have lost a great deal of blood and was possibly starting to go into shock. Got to get him warm and look at his wounds. I pulled our sleeping bags close to the fire for him.

We started to check his wounds. He had been badly mauled. I looked for spurting blood, which would indicate bleeding from an artery. His legs were uninjured. He had a large hole in his side under his right arm from the bear's paw. This required a large compress, which we had included in our first-aid kit.

I had sewn large game bags from unbleached muslin for this hunt. The material was new and clean. I tore the bags into long strips to use for bandages.

Al's head was very bloody—half of the skin on his forehead was missing, from the bottom half of his left eyebrow extending back into his hair. Due to all the blood and poor light, I did not notice part of the scalp was gone. I thought it had been torn back and was still attached.

I wrapped his head around and around several times with bandages which were quickly soaked with blood. His left arm was badly chewed, and the pain was very severe. He instructed me to take my knife and cut off the shredded piece of flesh that was hanging from the largest wound. There appeared to be a great deal of muscle and nerve damage.

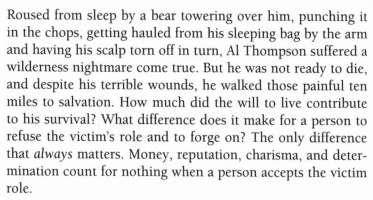

Roused from sleep by a bear towering over him, punching it in the chops, getting hauled from his sleeping bag by the arm and having his scalp torn off in turn, Al Thompson suffered a wilderness nightmare come true. But he was not ready to die, and despite his terrible wounds, he walked those painful ten miles to salvation. How much did the will to live contribute to his survival? What difference does it make for a person to refuse the victim's role and to forge on? The only difference that *always* matters. Money, reputation, charisma, and determination count for nothing when a person accepts the victim role.

J.L.

Leopard on the Rooftop

Pat James Byrne as told to
Captain John H. Brandt

Jadu Manji tried desperately to keep the tattered umbrella over the head of his wife Rongo as she attempted to shield her two-month-old infant from the incessant rain. The little family huddled under the eaves of a small rural bus stop near the village of Dharampur in Orissa state. The thatch provided little protection as the rain dripped down on them. It was late December and the night was cool. The soaking rain made everyone shiver as they crowded close together for warmth. No one else was at the stop, probably recognizing that travel on such a night had better be postponed until another day. The family had important business at Balliguda and both the man and his wife hoped the bus would come soon. At least inside the bus it would be dry.

The rain turned into a drizzle as the evening progressed and Jadu Manji handed his wife the umbrella, saying he needed to make a quick stop behind the hut before the bus arrived. Rongo smiled and told him to come right back. There was no one around and it was deathly quiet at the edge of the small village. Jadu Manji said he would only be a second and walked off into the darkness.

After several moments Rongo called out telling her husband to hurry. No answer came and Rongo wondered why her husband had gone so far from the hut. She called again, louder this time, but still no reply came. By now Rongo was becoming a bit annoyed as she pulled her shawl tighter about her and the baby. After several more minutes she stood up and went to the corner of the hut and shouted into the pitch black darkness telling Jadu Manji to be quick since she could hear the bus coming in the distance as it slithered along the muddy road to the village.

Rongo approached the driver as the bus came to a halt saying she and her husband were passengers but her husband had left and had not returned. Hearing what she had said, several of the bus passengers made rude jokes about her missing husband, and everyone laughed loudly when someone suggested that maybe he had gone off for a drink. Several inconsiderate passengers added that she should return to her village to locate her errant husband and not hold up the bus departure.

As the driver switched on his headlights, he could see a white, unidentified object lying on the track some fifty yards in front of the bus. Among the passengers was a man more knowledgeable than the rest who had been listening with growing concern to Rongo's tale. The man was a police officer and announcing his identity he ordered the bus driver to pull up to the white object to see what it was. Soon everyone could clearly see in the headlights that the object was a piece of white garment called a *chaddar*. There was a marked hush among the passengers as the police officer retrieved the item and all could clearly see that it was brightly stained with blotches of blood.

Calling Rongo to his side, he showed her the grisly discovery. She quickly identified it as the *chaddar* which her husband had been wearing when he disappeared. There was now no longer any question as to what had happened and several passengers came out to console Rongo who was screaming loudly in anguish and fear. It was a fear that gripped everyone and the police officer commanded all the passengers back into the bus for safety. Without a further word being said, everyone knew immediately that Jadu Manji had fallen victim to either a tiger or leopard and had been carried away in the darkness. There had been no sound. No cry for help. Death had been swiftly and skillfully executed. Knowing there was little further that could be accomplished, the police officer ordered the bus driver to proceed to the next station at Nuagam Post Office, taking the distraught wife and child along with them.

I was staying at a small bungalow at Nuagam at the time and, seeing the bus approach shortly after breakfast, I stepped off my verandah to see if my mail had been brought for me. It was still cold and wet outside and I carefully sidestepped or jumped over the many puddles of rain water still on the road as I approached the bus. A crowd of people had gathered and as they saw me a group split off running toward me. Everyone was shouting at once and I could make no sense of what they were saying. The police officer gave an authoritative command of silence and the group quickly shut up. Stepping forward, pulling the hysterical Rongo and her child with him, he proceeded to tell me what had happened at Dharampur the preceding night. Although no one was absolutely certain, everyone strongly suspected that a man-eater had carried off the missing man.

Questioning the crying woman was unproductive as all she could say was that Jadu Manji had walked off into the night saying he would be right back and had never returned. She had heard or seen nothing until they had discovered his bloody piece of clothing in the roadway after the arrival of the bus. Placing Rongo in the care of some relatives in the village,

I made immediate arrangements to return to the scene of the tragedy to see what I could discover regarding the mysterious disappearance.

Later that morning, upon the return of the mail bus, my tracker Budiya and I, accompanied by the headman of Nuagam, returned to Dharampur which we reached within a half-hour. In the bright sunshine, after the night's rain, the situation did not look nearly as ominous as it had in the dark of the night before. We started searching the sides of the road near where the bloodstained garment had been found.

Within a few minutes we located the pug marks of a large leopard in the muddy earth along the drain of the road embankment. We followed the tracks until we could see where the leopard had dug in when launching itself in the attack on its victim. Having made the kill, the leopard had dragged Jadu Manji along the side of the road. While being carried off, the bloody outer garment (found by the bus passengers on the road the night before) had fallen off Manji's body.

We were joined by a number of other village men eager to help find the body. The clearly visible drag mark, which soon diverged from the road bank, went up a small, wooded hill. Next to a large boulder which had provided some shelter, the leopard had laid down the body and commenced to eat. The grisly remains shocked many of the villagers who had never before seen a human kill made by a leopard. The man-eater had torn into the stomach cavity and had eaten a large portion of the lower abdomen as well as parts of the rib cage and a portion of the breast. We examined Jadu Manji's skull which quickly explained why there had been no outcry during the attack. Four large punctures on the back of the head, which had penetrated the cranium, indicated that the killer had struck his victim from behind and, with one bite to the head, had killed him. Thankfully, he died an instantaneous death and probably never knew what had befallen him.

I had planned to sit up over the corpse in the event the man-eater planned to return to consume what was left of his kill. However, shortly the police officials from Balliguda arrived at the scene guided by villagers. Since officialdom had preference, they removed the body, preventing any possibility of shooting the man-eater, even if he had returned. Unable to alter the situation, I returned to Nuagam village as well.

Several days went by with no further reported kills by the man-eater. It was during this time that two young men from Bodali village had gone off on a drinking party and were returning home from the Balliguda market. Since alcohol tends to exaggerate bravery as well as to dull common sense and good judgment, the two headed for home despite full knowledge of the man-eater being in the area. Upon reaching the banks of the Kalepin River, one of the drinking duet decided he was unable to proceed further and said he would lie down for a nap. Unable to carry his companion, the older man of the two decided to go on alone and planned to send someone back for his inebriated drinking partner as soon as he reached the village.

Upon reaching his home and explaining what had happened, the drunk was chastised for being out alone when he might well have become a victim of the man-eater. Several men soon left for the Kalepin River to bring the other man to the safety of the village. They carried axes and flaming torches to protect themselves and light their way in the dark jungle.

Reaching the spot on the river bank that had been identified to them, they searched and called but could find no one. In the light of the torches someone soon saw a glint of reflection from an axe next to an empty liquor bottle. No one said it out loud, but the realization of what might have happened entered several heads simultaneously. Spreading out, one of the men came across a blood-soaked *dhoti* which had belonged to the missing man. No further examination was required for the entire group to realize that the man-eater had claimed another victim. Knowing they could do nothing further to help, the two men ran as fast as possible to the village to alert everyone and make their gruesome discovery known. A larger group now quickly formed to return to the area to attempt to locate the body.

On the river bank, the tracks of a leopard were soon found. Lying nearby was a small, tin mirror case which was quickly identified as belonging to the missing man. Knowing that they could do little more in the dark and knowing the danger they themselves were in, the group returned to the village with the intention of resuming the search as soon as it was light enough to see.

I was still sound asleep that morning unaware of what had happened at Bodali village. A messenger pounded on my door, awakening me, and breathlessly informed me of what had happened to the drunken reveler the night before. Quickly dressing, I asked the messenger who was accompanied by some Bodali village men to return to the place of the kill, adding that I would join them as soon as I could get my gear together.

I had a bicycle for transportation and was shortly at the place where the road crossed the river. The men escorted me to where the mirror case and the *dhoti* cloth had been found. Strangely, we found tracks of both a tiger and a leopard which momentarily confused the search. Soon, however, I located the place where the death struggle had occurred. A large stain of blood still was visible and the tracks of the leopard were without question those of the killer. The tiger had only been an innocent traveler through the area either before or soon after the attack. The question remained: were these the tracks of the same leopard as the one who had killed Jadu Manji at the bus stop a few days before? It seemed likely that they were, since I'd never heard of two man-eaters operating in the same place at the same time.

While I contemplated the scene of the attack, a langur started calling from the nearby hillside. Some of the village men went to investigate and soon I heard shouts of, "Come quickly, Sahib!" Rushing to the site, we pushed through the circle of men who were staring at what little was left of the unfortunate man. As in the other killing, the man-eater had eaten part of the stomach, chest and viscera.

There was much flesh still remaining on the body and the village headman and I decided to attempt to sit up over the kill hoping that the man-eater would return. We sent my tracker and the men from the village back to the road to wait for us saying we would only stay until sundown. I told them to make noise on leaving so the leopard would think the entire group had departed.

We selected a comfortable spot at the base of a large thorn bush some forty yards up the hill from the body. We had a clear field of vision and I felt the thorn bush would give us reasonable protection from an unwanted attack from the rear.

We only intended to stay as long as there was sufficient light to shoot since I had not brought a flashlight with me and also did not relish a nighttime sit-up on the ground with the man-eater about. About a half-hour before sundown we began to hear clearly audible noises coming from our left, quickly closing the distance between us. We were amazed the man-eater would be so reckless as to approach in this manner, apparently taking no precaution whatsoever. I had never before experienced such an audacious killer as this and gripped my rifle knowing that in a moment the killer would reach the dead man's body. Its approach grew louder and louder. Anytime a man-eater comes to a kill it is always a moment of extreme tension and excitement. Every nerve in my body was taut. Every sense was alert. Then the large, dark body of an animal came into view making directly for the kill. I slowly placed the gun to my shoulder. Then the adrenaline rapidly drained as I looked at a wild pig rather than the leopard!

Knowing that the villagers would have never accepted the abhorrent possibility of a pig desecrating the dead body, I had no choice but to kill the animal which fell dead at the first shot.

Within moments I heard the excited shouting of my tracker and the villagers as they scurried up the hill anticipating the death of the man-eater. I knew they would be disappointed but the circumstances were such that there was no other alternative. It was a quiet and dejected group that returned to the village that night carrying with it the remains of the latest victim for proper burial.

On January 11th, I was called from my home late in the afternoon by a villager on a bicycle imploring me to quickly follow him to the burial ground near Nuagam. He had been on his way to town and had seen a leopard brazenly exhuming a body in broad daylight. He insisted that if we hurried we might still find him there. I found all this a bit hard to believe but quickly slung my rifle over my shoulder and we pedaled as fast as we could to the place where he had seen the leopard. We parked the bicycles and quietly approached the burial site concealed by a small hedge. Peering cautiously over the top, I was amazed to see the leopard still pawing the ground not more than fifty yards away. I sighted over the hedge and fired a shot. The leopard spun about and made one gigantic leap and was gone.

Hearing the shot, several men joined us; although we searched diligently, it soon became too dark to see and we did not find the leopard. Returning the next morning, we resumed the search again, going a bit further into the bush, looking hopefully for blood spoor which, until then, had eluded us. With no signs to guide us, we were amazed when, quite by accident, we stumbled across the body of the dead animal. Regretfully, it had been found before we arrived by a hyena which had managed to gnaw on the body and had consumed quite a bit of it. Although this was disappointing, the highlight of the discovery was that the leopard, which was a big male, had a large number of festering porcupine quills deeply imbedded in its left forefoot. The quills must have caused the animal great pain and would certainly have handicapped it in pursuit of normal prey. This, coupled with the fact that the leopard had been attempting to exhume a human body, left little doubt that this was the man-eater. So much for optimistic and hasty conclusions that would soon almost cost us our lives.

January 12th dawned as another gloomy, rainy day, but since we felt we now had effectively taken care of the man-eater problem, I was pleased when the mid-day bus brought in a visitor to break the monotony of a long, lonely day. The man coming to my bungalow proved to be the schoolmaster from a larger village called Gunjibada which lies about five miles up the road from Dharampur. The man, Surja Singh, informed me that a tiger had killed a milk cow belonging to an elderly widow living in a tiny forest hamlet called Sandrekia. He had been asked by the people of the village to see if he could request my help in killing the animal. Listening to the description, I felt that the matter of shooting a cattle-killing tiger would be quite routine and, not having any other commitments, I told him I would be pleased to help. I borrowed a 12-gauge shotgun and some heavy L.G. shells and, accompanied by my tracker Budiya, we caught the mid-day bus to Dharampur. After leaving the bus and before beginning our walk to the hamlet, I started to organize my gear and discovered that my 5-cell flashlight, upon which I was entirely dependent for nighttime shooting, had been left on the bus accidentally. There was little we could do except continue our walk toward Sandrekia, although I felt that now the situation totally favored the tiger rather than us. I had with me a rustic lantern with a headlight reflector that been left behind by American troops serving in India during the war. It was far from adequate but, under the circumstances, the best we had available. Budiya and I decided to give it a try, although we were not very optimistic.

Following Surja Singh's directions, we walked along a swiftly flowing mountain stream and soon, after a strenuous climb, reached the tiny hamlet which consisted of all of three huts. Sandrekia was certainly no metropolis but, because of its size, it didn't take long to find where the cow had been pulled down. The kill, we were told, was lying under a small hut located on a hillside a short distance from the village. A frail woman holding a small infant to her bosom volunteered to show us to the place and then added that she was the owner of the dead cow. She was visibly moved as she told us that this was the last animal of three that she had owned and that now she would be thrown upon the mercy of relatives to support her since the tiger had now killed her last surviving animal.

The structure where the cow had been killed was a corral made of sturdy planks buried upright in the ground as a wall. On top of this was a bamboo frame covered with grass which served as a roof. I examined the dead cow and the surroundings and quickly determined that the killer was a leopard rather than a tiger. The woman begged me to rid them of the killer and stressed that it made little difference to her if the cow had died on the fangs of a leopard or a tiger. Knowing the desperate situation that existed at Sandrekia, I agreed to do what I could to shoot the beast.

Urging the villagers to return to their homes down the hill, Budiya and I dragged the cow outside of the enclosure; we then decided that in the absence of a suitable tree we would start our vigil on the fragile roof of the cow pen. This gave us little security since it was only about five feet high, but it was the best we could arrange. We placed a blind of straw in front of us to partially shield our movements and give me a chance to get my rifle in shooting position should the leopard return. It soon turned cold as the sun went down, and we pulled our jacket collars up to protect us from the breeze that now blew with considerable force down the hillside.

All was quiet and we heard no sounds for the first two hours after sundown. Quite suddenly our tranquility was shattered by a violent push from underneath the bamboo roofing upon which we were seated. The unexpected jolt was a surprise we hadn't expected and since we had heard or seen nothing, we moved our position a bit to see if we could peer into the cow pen to see what had happened, somehow knocking loose a board that fell from the roof into the interior of the pen. A blood curdling roar, followed by a deep snarl immediately below us, brought instant realization that the leopard had managed to sneak into the enclosure without alerting us and had tried, unsuccessfully, to reach us through the roof. It was a most unpleasant situation to be in, but it was quickly brought to resolution when the leopard made a bound over the outer wall of the corral and disappeared.

Budiya and I decided that our vantage point wasn't the safest place to sit in the dark since the leopard now knew our position and might make a more successful stalk the next time if he should try again. We took our headlamp and, walking very cautiously through the darkness, proceeded to a small hut nearby thinking that perhaps it would offer more security for us than the first. Reaching the hut we went inside and Budiya lit a small fire. We found, to our dismay, that the door to the hut could not be properly closed and that only a fragile stick was propped against it to keep it from swinging open.

Budiya, who had been quite shaken by our recent visit by the leopard, commented that in view of the aggressive behavior of the animal he fully believed it was the man-killer, and that the leopard we had shot a few days earlier with the porcupine quills in its foot had not been the man-eater after all. I was inclined to agree since our recent nocturnal visitor was abnormally unafraid of people and seemed determined to add a new victim to its list.

While discussing this possibility, we heard a soft movement against the door. It sounded almost like someone knocking to request permission to enter. For a moment we thought perhaps some hillmen, having seen us, were seeking shelter for the night. I flashed on my headlamp and directed the beam toward the door. It suddenly became obvious that something was trying to enter and that the tapping was caused by the door being pushed inward against the small stick which we had propped against it. We both came to the chilling realization that our visitor was the leopard trying again to reach us!

Being unsuccessful in opening the door, the leopard moved around the hut examining it for other means of entry. We listened carefully and I motioned for Budiya to pick up a large boulder in the corner of the hut, which had been used for a fireplace, and place it securely against the door.

Budiya and I sat in complete silence attempting to interpret sounds from outside as to what the leopard was doing. Our reverie came to a quick end as we heard the leopard jump onto the roof of the hut. Quickly this was followed by dust showering down on us accompanied by scratching and tearing sounds as the leopard attempted to make a hole through which he could enter the hut. There was now no longer any question that this was the man-eater!

The leopard, as if contemplating his next move, paused for a moment and I took this opportunity to switch on the light thinking that his attack had progressed to the point that the light would in no way now deter the leopard from his intended purpose of killing us. Through the roof I could see the extended paw of the killer as he was enlarging the hole in the thatch. Budiya gave a yell and the leopard, momentarily startled, withdrew his paw and stuck his head through the opening to survey the situation and perhaps look over his intended meal.

The leopard was only a few feet above my head and I could have touched him with the barrel tip. Before this unsurpassed opportunity to kill the man-eater could fade, I pulled the trigger at point blank range. The leopard slumped backward from the velocity of the shot, but did not fall off the roof. There was no sound and we felt sure he was dead. Walking carefully outside we could see the spotted form lying on the roof of the hut. The shotgun blast, directly in his face, had been more than the man-eater could take.

Early the next morning, some village men helped carry the leopard back to Nuagam. There was jubilation in Sandrekia and Dharampur and everyone felt they could now resume a normal way of life again without the constant fear of imminent and horrible death.

While skinning this man-eater, I found that he also had been partially handicapped by having a number of porcupine quills imbedded in his forepaws. Walking must have been indeed painful for him. However, the decisive factor as to why he had turned into a man-eater was an old gunshot wound in his right shoulder. It had obviously crippled him to the point that he could no longer hunt properly and had turned to humans as his easiest source of food. There was no doubt that he was the dreaded man-eater and no more human deaths were reported in the area.

To my chagrin, I found that, since I had not killed the leopard actively over a human kill, under existing law I could not claim the government reward. The gratitude of the village was, however, more than adequate compensation.

This tale provides us another look at the great white hunter of colonial India. Legend has elevated him to such rank that you'd think his kind were all wealthy colonels living in splendor. Heralded by bugles, this gentleman hero would foray on elephants to the danger zone, dismount on a golden ladder, and through some magnificent blend of personal steel and shaman's magic face down the terrible man-eater and drop it with a single shot. But here comes Pat James Byrne on his bicycle, a shotgun in one hand and a flashlight in the other. These items are modest tackle for the job, but not as modest as the manner in which Byrne relates his tale.

Byrne tracks the man-eater to the disemboweled body of a local man. He knows the cat will return that evening to feed on the corpse, but there is no cover, and, having lost his flashlight, Byrne does "not relish a nighttime sit-up on the ground with the man-eater about." Relish? Try to picture a more appalling job. The leopard does not show that evening, but Byrne, undaunted, works out another ambush and, with a Indian companion, sits on the roof of a flimsy, five-foot-high cow pen and waits. The leopard is so crafty that it sneaks into the very pen Byrne is "tranquilly" sitting on and slashes up at the bamboo ceiling, trying to get at him. The hunter finds himself in "a most unpleasant situation," he says. Byrne doesn't get a shot, but a few days later, he finds himself in that creaky hut with a stick against the door and a savage leopard trying to force entry. The cat jumps onto the roof and starts tearing at the thatch, beginning to rip a hole through which he can enter the hut. Byrne waits until the man-eater puts "his head through the opening to survey the situation and perhaps look over his intended meal." The cat is so close that Byrne can touch its face with the barrel of his shotgun. "I pulled the trigger at point-blank range," Byrne adds casually. For his effort, Byrne gets jobbed out of the government reward because the man-eater was not killed while devouring a human being. Pat James Byrne could only hop back on his bicycle and peddle for home, not richer by a single rupee, but feeling that "the gratitude of the village was . . . more than adequate compensation."

Maybe the fabled status of the great white hunter is well earned after all.

J.L.

Grizzly Attack

Stephen Herrero

On September 11, 1973, Al Johnson, a game biologist with the state of Alaska, cautiously approached a grizzly bear mother with three cubs in Mt. McKinley National Park. He went to the park to photograph moose, but the chance to photograph the bear family seemed too good to pass by. For about three hours he photographed the bears, never coming closer than one hundred yards. He was downwind of them and quiet, and so he felt sure that they were unaware of his presence. By late afternoon the light began to fade, and he concluded that his 1000-mm lens wouldn't get good pictures. Also, the bears were moving away from him and into an area where there were no good trees to climb. At this point Johnson climbed what he thought was a safe, sturdy tree. He took his 105-mm and 300-mm lenses with him, hoping for close-ups. From about ten to fifteen feet up the tree he began making squeaking sounds like a rabbit in order to draw the bears closer. At first only the cubs were interested, but after about five minutes of squeaking the mother bear looked up and headed in an arc toward the tree. Johnson described what happened next in an interview given to Larry Kaniut:

I stopped calling and started taking pictures. At about 50 yards distant I yelled at her, hoping to impress upon her that I was man. My yelling didn't cause any visible reaction. Some 30 to 40 yards out she looked back to the cubs. If there were any vocal signals, I never heard them; but the cubs then held back and followed the sow in some 30 yards behind her.

When she was about 20 yards out, she had increased her speed to a slow gallop; and at that point I recorded a blurred image on film. Either because things started happening so fast or because of my state of mind, my images of some events aren't real sharp.

Because of the lower limbs I could hear the sow when she arrived at the tree base. She hit my pack and continued on beyond the tree another 10 to 15 yards before she stopped and looked back towards the cubs, which by this time were stopped a similar distance from the tree but on the opposite side from her and in full view of me.

When I glanced at the sow, I realized she was confused—wanting to run but not wanting to leave the cubs. Like a young, dedicated, foolish photographer, I was trying to focus on the three standing cubs. I remember thinking, "What a fantastic photo!" Unfortunately, I never pushed the shutter button for about then a cub let out a bawl which instantly sent the sow for my tree.

I felt the tree shake violently. When I looked down, I saw her head and shoulders. The next thing I knew, I was being pulled from the tree. Evidently she had enough momentum and claw power to carry her up to my boot, for that is what she got hold of. I got the impression that had I been up the tree another foot or had I held fast to the tree, she would not have gotten me. The tree diameter at the butt was close to eight inches, and I was roughly 15 feet up; but until I return to measure, I'll never know for sure. . . .

I had held both arms in front of my face for protection. I pushed once with one leg but decided it was fruitless and I'd best not get her mad. She bit each arm three or four times and made a few lacerations in my scalp with her claws. Fortunately she had the safety of the cubs on her mind and wasn't a hundred percent bent on getting me.

After I pushed with one leg, I had my eyes closed except once when I looked up and saw her standing with mouth agape, arms open with claws exposed—just like a "live mount" one sees in a museum with the exception that she was looking to one side.

After she bit into my right elbow a good one, she grabbed my right shoulder and raised me off the ground a couple of feet. When she let go, I turned a little and came down on my stomach (just after I got on my stomach I remember thinking, "I hope she hurries and gets it over with").

I then pulled my head in and clasped the back of my neck with my hands to give some protection to my head and neck. Earlier I was reluctant to roll to my stomach since I knew that would expose my head. I knew that bears have a tendency to go for the head.

Though she worked me over only a short while, it seemed like ages.

She next bit the small of my back but couldn't get much of a bite because of my heavy clothing and because of the concave surface. She then stepped forward and bit my head.

I remember hearing what sounded like the crushing of bone and wondered why I did not die or at least pass out. Come to find out she had only removed a strip of scalp, and it was the scraping of her teeth against my skull and not the crushing of bone that I had heard. As I said earlier, I don't remember any pain.

She evidently figured I wouldn't give her any more problem for I heard her leave in the direction I vaguely remember the cubs moving. Right away I got up and headed towards the road, which was roughly 300 yards distant. I turned and looked back once, but I couldn't see much.

My right eye was swollen shut and I could only see out of my left by holding my head higher than normal. I pulled my coat hood over my head and held my right arm tight against my body to reduce bleeding. I lay down twice to rest before I made the road. Fortunately I lay on the road less than a minute before two vehicles came along.

Help did arrive soon, including a paramedic who bandaged Johnson's wounds. Johnson was airlifted to Fairbanks:

The nurses told me that I was a bloody mess and that they spent over three hours in the emergency room cutting my hair and clothes, and cleaning me for surgery.

Two doctors worked me over, transplanted some skin from my thigh to my head, patched the torn main artery in my right shoulder and sewed shut some cuts on my head. The puncture wounds on my arms were left open to drain and heal.

One doctor told me that the paramedic from Healy probably saved my life by stopping the flow of blood—they put four pints of blood into me before I went to surgery.

After two weeks in the hospital and some fine treatment by the nurses, doctors, my girlfriend, who is now my wife, and friends, I recovered almost to prior condition.

The grizzly bear family was not shot or held to blame for the incident. The bears were known to be in the area of the encounter for about a week prior to the mauling, but no other aggressive incidents had occurred.

Along with the polar bear, the grizzly is North America's most formidable land animal. Like black bears and brown bears, the grizzly is quite willing to give its life to protect its cubs. A human's presence anywhere near a grizzly cub can almost ensure some kind of response from the sow, which was illustrated when Al Johnson heard "the scraping of her teeth against my skull." That a game biologist such as Johnson did not understand the grizzlies patterns is probably the wrong conclusion. His near-fatal error was in believing that a hulking grizzly sow could not climb a tree. Given the power and ferocity of grizzlies, I consider Johnson the luckiest attack victim in this book. Perhaps the bear was more concerned with protecting her cubs and leading them to safety than in killing Johnson.

Travels in grizzly country are always a bit risky. Aside from warnings to try to stay in open terrain in the hopes of seeing the grizzly before it sees you, there is virtually nothing a traveler can do to ensure that he or she won't accidentally encounter the animal. Of course, an encounter does not automatically mean an attack; in fact, the odds are greatly against it. The previous story, however, shows the gravity of the situation when the odds run out and the great bear strikes.

J.L.

The Dasingabadi Rogue

Pat James Byrne as told to
Captain John H. Brandt

It was early on a Sunday morning in April of 1953. The days were becoming oppressively hot, and Augostino, a lay Catholic preacher, decided to leave early to avoid the heat on his mile walk to the village of Dasingabadi. He was pleased with his accomplishments in that two families from the hamlet had already converted to Catholicism. As he walked, he went over in his mind what he would include in the sermon that Sunday morning.

The Pangali Ghat road that led from his house to Dasingabadi wound through some dense forest in a hilly section. The thick overhanging boughs made a shaded arch and gave a pleasant coolness to the road. Although there were tiger and leopard about, there had been no problem for quite some time and Augostino had no fears as he started into the forested area.

Reaching the summit of a small hill he saw some distance ahead of him an elephant feeding on the roadside. Augostino was not alarmed because elephant were often encountered and moved away quickly after sensing that a man was approaching. As he watched he felt a cool breeze hit the nape of his neck which, within seconds, carried his scent to the elephant. Then the unanticipated and abnormal happened. The elephant jerked its head on catching the tart human scent and raising its trunk started ambling up wind on the roadway directly toward Augostino. As Augostino turned to escape, the elephant let out an earsplitting trumpet and broke into a run after the fleeing man. Although an elephant may appear bulky and ungainly, on an open course he can easily outrun a man. It took only a moment for him to close the distance between himself and the desperate, dodging preacher. The elephant raised his trunk and with one horrifying swipe, like a man crushing a fly with a fly-swatter, he knocked Augostino off his feet and sent him sprawling into the roadside ditch. Stunned and unable to move, the man saw the elephant loom above him and then kneel on him before all went mercifully black. The enraged elephant tore the crushed and flattened remains into pieces and then, following a mysterious ritual incomprehensible to man, proceeded to cover the mangled remains with branches and leaves. Still grumbling to himself, the elephant then turned and disappeared into the dense undergrowth.

Ordinarily, this horrible scenario would have been pieced together later from the physical evidence at the scene. However, in this case, there had been a horrified witness who had watched the entire episode from a nearby hillside.

Ananda was a woodcutter from the village of Pangali who had gone to the forest that day to retrieve a few *sal* logs that he had illegally cut a few days earlier. He felt, since it was a Sunday, that most likely the forest guard would be taking a day off and he would be relatively safe from being caught. What he saw that morning was not a part of his plans and, after regaining his wits, he hesitated for a moment wondering what he should do. If he reported the killing he would compromise his reason for having been in the woods. After assuring himself that the elephant was now gone and he could see or hear no further movement in the area, he decided he had no choice but to make his grisly discovery known and let the authorities know what he had witnessed. As quickly as he could run, he headed for Pangali to report the matter to his headman. Quickly realizing the seriousness of the situation and the imminent possibility that someone else might be killed, the headman ordered Ananda to run to Dasingabadi to alert the police officer stationed there.

Listening to his tale, the police officer in charge decided that, since it was now late afternoon, little could be accomplished before daylight and requested that Ananda remain at the station overnight so he could lead a rescue party to the scene of the tragedy the next day.

Late the next morning, as plans were being completed for a group to proceed to the Pangali Ghat road, a trio of highly excited men ran up to the steps of the police station shouting that an elephant had just attacked the Revenue Bungalow at Dasingabadi and had killed the watchman. They had come as quickly as possible to report the incident which had occurred at 10:00 A.M. that morning. With the news from Ananda of the preacher's death the preceding day, it appeared most likely that the same rogue had continued his murderous escapade and had continued on to wreak mayhem at the bungalow which was not far from where the first killing had occurred.

The group, led by two police officers carrying old, obsolete rifles, entirely inadequate to stop an elephant, moved cautiously and apprehensively toward the area where the woodcutter said he had seen the killing take place.

Entering the darkened forest area, they saw some distance ahead of them a brush pile in the middle of the road. As they came closer it quickly became apparent from the smell of decaying flesh that this was the funerary shroud of branches and leaves which Ananda had seen the elephant place on top of his victim. Kicking the branches aside, they saw beneath it the fly-encrusted, bloated and blackened body parts of Augostino that the elephant had mangled and mashed virtually beyond recognition. The sight sickened the entire group and it was only with considerable determination that the remains were gingerly placed into a sack to be transported back to Dasingabadi.

With great haste the rescue party trotted back to the bungalow where the second reported killing had occurred. Arriving at the bungalow, the two policemen reported in to the senior police inspector who was already on the scene. The policemen described what they had found; the inspector motioned them to the back of the building where they again saw an identical mound of branches. They did not have to be told that it would also contain the same crushed fragments of a human being, much as they had found on the roadway. The watchman's corpse, or what remained of it, was also removed and turned over to relatives for cremation.

While they were completing their investigation and talking with the villagers, a man bicycled up to the bungalow with a report that another killing had occurred the previous night at a place about ten miles from the Bungalow. The police learned that a man from the village of Sakerbadi had not returned home the previous evening. Not knowing about any of the other killings, the villagers had waited until daylight and then had walked up the track that they felt the man would have used on his return home. They shouted his name loudly but received no reply. Soon they too found a pile of branches on the trail permeated by the same sickeningly sweet odor of decomposing flesh. The buzzing of the flies around the brush pile left no doubt that they had found the body of the missing man. Just then above them on the hillside they heard the loud trumpeting call of an elephant, and in one movement the entire group fled the scene leaving the body where they had found it. The headman had ordered one man with a bicycle to go to Dasingabadi, by a long circuitous route, to advise the authorities of the killing.

The police were now extremely concerned. Three deaths in a twenty-four-hour period, presumably all the murderous work of one elephant, prompted them to contact the District Officer (Collector) to request his authorization to declare the animal a rogue, which, as a public nuisance and danger, should be destroyed immediately. The D.O. wasted no time in issuing the required proclamation and invited interested hunters to come and undertake the task of killing the animal.

Almost a month had passed since the killings had occurred before I heard of the incidents. A telegram had been sent to my home in Calcutta by the headman of Nuagam requesting my assistance if I could get away. He said others had attempted to kill the rogue but all had been unsuccessful. I made plans to go look at the situation, although at that time even getting to Dasingabadi was a major undertaking. The village lay almost forty miles from Nuagam, which is where any road worthy of the name ended. Beyond Nuagam the only means of transport was by walking or, if available, by bicycle. On my way, I contacted the District Officer who issued me a permit to shoot the rogue and also kindly gave me a letter of introduction to all police units in the area asking for their assistance and cooperation, which proved to be most helpful to me.

With the aid of the headman I hired six men at Nuagam to help me transport my camp gear and equipment. I bicycled but often thought that perhaps walking would have been much wiser. It took several days to reach Dasingabadi where we arrived on the morning of May 26th.

The villagers were elated at my arrival and quickly told me that the rogue was still in the area, and that only three weeks earlier he had attacked a caravan of bullock carts hauling logs. He had smashed two carts, killing the bullocks

who were unable to escape his attack. Although the cart dri-
vers had escaped injury, an innocent villager, who just happened to be in the right place at the wrong time, had not
been so fortunate. The enraged elephant had caught him in
his trunk and smashed his body into a pulp against the base
of a tree.

The police at Dasingabadi confirmed the event, and they
and the villagers helped me bring my gear to the Revenue
Bungalow where I would stay. It was a bit disconcerting
knowing that the rogue I was after had attacked the very
building where I was to sleep and had killed the watchman
there only a few weeks earlier on the first day of his rampage.
One of the men who was assisting with the gear broke away
from the group and came over to me. He was small and wiry
and had a huge grin on his face as he saluted me. Speaking
very quietly, as a jungle man should, he introduced himself as
Bana. He added that he was the village Shikari and would be
my guide and assistant in hunting the elephant. Glancing
over his shoulder at the police officers, he added that he was
also the village poacher and knew the jungle well. With great
confidence he said that he had no fear of elephants and, if we
were to team up, we could soon slay the rogue. I liked his demeanor and sincerely hoped he was right.

Since the attack on the log carts almost a month earlier,
there had been no reports of the elephant, and no other
known killings had occurred. As the days went by without
any reports, it was difficult not to entertain thoughts that perhaps the elephant had moved away, or died, or changed his
habits. All were unlikely, but the frustrating inactivity of
waiting made me wonder if I had made a mistake in setting
up my headquarters in Dasingabadi. Hunting of rogues is always an exercise in patience, and I did my best to familiarize
myself with the area and to keep occupied while awaiting
news of another attack by the monster.

Bana and I examined numerous old spoor, presumably of
the rogue, in the jungles surrounding Dasingabadi. None

were fresh but, from the easily visible tracks in the soft dirt near where the bungalow guard had been killed, we estimated the size of the bull at about ten feet tall. The rogue was a huge animal and one of obviously enormous strength. Unfortunately, diligent searching, day after day, produced no fresh tracks or signs of the elephant in the vicinity. Another week went by and my time was running out. I had almost decided that unless some report came in within another day or two I would start the return trip to Nuagam. Then the next day, what I had been awaiting happened!

A messenger brought a letter to the bungalow from the police officer stationed at a village called Bamnigam, which was located almost twenty-four miles from Dasingabadi. The letter contained a detailed description of a killing by an elephant in the area a few days earlier. The fact that the killer had placed a mound of boughs over his victim confirmed that it must be the same rogue who obviously covered great distances in his travels. I debated on what the best course of action might be since it would take me a day or two, at best, to reach Bamnigam. Bana and Boliar Singh, the headman, discussed the situation with me and said that from their past experience the rogue rotated at fairly frequent intervals throughout his range. Since he had been away from Dasingabadi for several weeks, it might be possible that we would be on his circuit, and he would likely soon return. I knew they were also concerned about my leaving which meant they would be left to face the rogue alone without weapons. We agreed to stay another few days to see what happened since the news of the killing from Bamnigam was now already several days old. It proved to be a wise decision. It was now June 3rd.

The day was one which would long be remembered by me, as well as all the local villagers, because an enormous storm crossed the area that night causing extreme damage to homes and trees. For a time I wondered if the bungalow would survive the lashing rain and cyclone-force winds. About midnight the storm abated somewhat, and when morning arrived I could see trees uprooted all around the compound. A large mango tree had blown over on the roadway, and a number of village women were already there with baskets retrieving the mangos which now were suddenly so conveniently within reach. There was much talking and laughing outside from all the people when suddenly a loud shriek of fear from the women quickly brought me to the verandah to see what had happened. Wanting to be prepared for any emergency, I automatically grabbed the .470 Express rifle propped next to my bed. Stepping onto the verandah I was thankful for this intuitive action because on the roadway was the very creature I had spent so many weeks waiting for. It was as if destiny had arranged this introduction with the rogue on my doorstep! I motioned Bana to remain indoors as I stepped into the yard.

The bull, a huge tusker, was still some three hundred yards away, and, since the wind was blowing toward me, he had not yet scented or seen me. He was also still somewhat distracted by all the scurrying villagers who had run at the first indication of his presence. He had made no attempt to catch anyone, and, after moving a few yards toward the bungalow, he veered to the left and disappeared into the brush. There was now total silence. Every villager had disappeared, presumably to the questionable safety of their frail huts.

I was now alone and proceeded one step at a time toward the area where I had last seen the elephant. I tested the wind constantly hoping it would not change direction and alert the rogue to my presence before I had seen him. It took me several moments to proceed one hundred yards but I could make out no sound or sight of the bull.

Suddenly there was a loud crash to my rear, and I swirled, fully convinced that I had passed the bull and that he was making an attack from ambush behind me. What I saw was hardly what I expected! The bull had silently walked through the underbrush and, apparently unaware of me, had entered the compound. The crash I heard was the spectacle of the bull demolishing the roof of the two-room bungalow. He had grabbed a roof timber and with a shaking tug had torn loose the entire end of the roof. Although he could have now easily seen me, he was so engrossed with his demolition project that he totally ignored my approach. I had closed the distance between us to about twenty-five yards when the bull suddenly stopped and became deathly silent. He raised his trunk and picking up my scent, swirled in a lightning-like turn, and thundered across the small compound toward me. His charge came as no surprise. I had expected it and was prepared.

Before the bull had taken three steps, the heavy bullet from the left barrel slammed into his forehead stopping him in mid-stride. He sank to his knees with a jolt as I fired the second barrel. With a shudder he then rolled quietly onto his side and lay still.

I carefully approached the great tusker, but there was no question that he was dead. I sat on his head catching my breath over the excitement of the past few minutes waiting for my pulse rate to return to normal.

My cook and Bana soon appeared from inside the partially-wrecked bungalow and joined me. Within moments, calls of curious inquiry came from the jungle in several directions asking, "Sahib, is he dead? Is it safe to come out?" Assuring them that the rogue was dead, we were soon surrounded by a deliriously happy group of villagers. Some men brought a chair in which they insisted I be seated so they could put me on their shoulders to dance in triumph with me through the village. I made it on my precarious perch through the festivity which lasted until late into the night. Although neither I nor the villagers would ever determine what had prompted the great tusker to take on such murderous and abnormal pathological behavior, no one really cared. The Dasingabadi rogue was dead!

———◆———

Again we journey to faraway India to join Pat James Byrne peddling to Dasingabadi on his rusty bicycle. When Byrne quips that "it was a bit disconcerting to know that the rogue I was after had attacked the very building where I was to sleep and had killed the watchman there only a few weeks earlier," we know instantly how King Shahryar felt as Scheherezade bewitched him with her thousand and one tales. The romance, the exotic remoteness, the peril, the very name Dasingabadi, combined with the understatement of Byrne's delivery, transport us much as the Jinn transported El Sindbad, Ali Baba, and countless others to enchanted lands. Thus so do we feel, transported by Byrne to a land of veiled princesses, snake charmers, sages, and killer elephants.

Killer elephants? To most Americans, the concept of a rogue elephant is not as much a fact as a sort of enchantment.

In that fateful building, we hook up with Byrne and "Bana," the fearless village poacher whose demeanor and enthusiasm the hunter so admires. Through a hundred turns we follow Byrne until he's closed the distance between himself and the rogue "to about twenty-five yards . . . when the bull suddenly . . . raised his trunk and picking up my scent, swirled in a lightning-like turn and thundered across the small compound toward me." Byrne has done it again: he has faced death at point-blank range. Naturally, he says, "His charge came as no surprise. I had expected it and was prepared." Only a perfect shot will deliver Byrne, and the district, from the "great tusker." Of course, Byrne delivers; "the Dasingabadi rogue is dead!"

Most experts feel that a rogue elephant is a product of some sort form of dementia or distemper. Whatever the cause, a genuine rogue is a true rarity. Aggressive behavior by elephants is well known, however. That elephants are smart and trainable enough to be beasts of burden does not mean that elephants without such training will behave like the domesticated tuskers in a Ringling Brothers performance. The elephant's only enemy is man, simply because no other animal is foolish enough to challenge its great size and strength. In the wild, elephants do what they want, when they want, and where they want. As most agree, elephants are best enjoyed from a distance, preferably from a jeep that can provide swift escape if necessary.

J.L.

I Will Save You!

Peter Hathaway Capstick

Man-eaters are among the most fascinating and dangerous animals, a point driven home by the story of an African game warden in the area of Mala Mala, a private game reserve in South Africa near the Kruger Park in the Transvaal.

He is Elfas Mbungla, a Shangaan tribesman married to a woman named Vina. It was March of 1981 and Elfas had been on leave with his twenty-three-year-old wife but decided to return to work a day early. Walking through the bush, they hoofed it back to within five miles of the Mala Mala reserve before blackness began to fall, stopping at a hut on the Sand River to spend the night. It was a standard thatched affair but had a bed and mattress, an odd length of metal pipe, a few empty soft-drink bottles, and a working kerosene lamp with a nearly full reservoir. A "trail hut" for the use of the wardens, it was comfortable enough, and Vina went out to collect firewood while the thirty-five-year-old Elfas, a slender, lightly built man, puttered around waiting for Vina to return.

His wife's shriek broke his thoughts. A lioness, old, decrepit, and desperate, had caught the woman and lay atop her, having severely bitten her thighs and buttocks. Vina never knew where the lioness had come from but managed to get an arm up to protect her head, an arm that the starving lioness badly crushed between her rotting and broken teeth. She was the rare but classic man-eater, too savage with starvation and injury to fear attacking man.

Elfas Mbungla was out of the half-door in one movement, his hand clutching the first weapon that came within reach. It was a well-worn broom. Running toward the sound of Vina's screams, he came on the twilight scene and smacked the lioness over the back until the broom handle splintered. Refusing to leave the wounded woman, the lioness ignored him but for furious snarls. In a growing panic, Elfas dashed back to the hut and loaded up with empty bottles, rocks, and anything else he could find to throw. Incredibly, the lioness melted off into the dark bush. Dragging the mauled Vina, Elfas managed to get back into the hut and slam the flimsy door.

Elfas had a hard look in the low light at Vina's wounds, which were severe but not fatal. As he tried to figure out what to do, a low rumble came from the now open door. The lioness stood there, her mouth open, having returned to collect her meal.

Mbungla lunged for the piece of pipe and swung it as hard as he could at the lioness' head. He missed. To his horror, the door collapsed under the impact of the pipe. With growing terror, he heard his wife ask through her pain if she was going to die. "I will save you," answered Elfas, but one wonders if he believed it at the time.

Thinking in overdrive, Elfas recalled the kerosene lamp and the heavy overcoat he wore against the chill of the autumn March evening. Ripping the coat into strips, he soaked them in kerosene—locally called paraffin—lit them, and flipped them at the threatening lioness. Snarling, the big cat withdrew for a few moments.

Having inadvertently smashed the door with the pipe, Elfas

snatched the mattress off the bed and tried to jam the opening with it. All was quiet outside as he stuffed a pair of pillows into the windows, sealing them with scraps left over from the coat. Elfas didn't know it as he mixed some salt into water to treat his wife's wounds, but fifteen hours would pass before the nightmare of the man-eater would be over.

A rasping snarl and pawstroke shocked him upright over the moaning body of Vina as the remains of the coat were torn from the window frame. So starving was the lioness that she actually ate the green-beige overcoat, buttons and all. Sure that his number was up, Elfas let his mind race over how to save his wife. Although the hut didn't have a high roof, Elfas tore a hole in the thatch and shoved his wife through it. Vina was too badly injured to hang in place by herself, so Elfas used his belt to secure her to the outer rafters, expecting to die fighting the lioness below.

The hours crawled by, blackness tinted with the groans and snarls of the lioness as she kept returning. In one of her assaults, she ate kapok-filled pillows that had been stuffed into a window. Every few minutes, the rasp of claws on dry grass paralyzed the couple, but Elfas began to realize that the large overhang of the thatch roof offered insufficient support for the lioness, so she could not reach them, shivering under the starlight.

Dawn broke as a mango tint in the east. There was no sight or sign of the lioness, but Elfas and his wife slipped from the roof and crossed the river to prevent the cat from following them up. By this time, Elfas was completely mute, his voice gone from shouting at the lioness all night long.

It was six months before woodcutters found the desiccated body of the lioness, well processed by hyenas and vultures, apparently starved to death by her failure to kill and eat one or both of the Mbunglas. The morning after the attack, the spoor of the lioness had been wiped away by a sudden rain, but the tattered remains of the cat indicated that she had died shortly after the attack on the couple. Fluffy kapok from the eaten pillows and shreds of Elfas' coat were littered near the bones, some particles windblown into the thornbushes. The lioness, from the informal postmortem, had been so desperate that she had eaten a porcupine. The teeth of the sun-whitened skull were broken, worn, and diseased, and only one claw was found near the scavenger-ravaged carcass. It was mounted in silver and presented to Elfas Mbungla by—who else—Gary Player. Elfas Mbungla is now the head warden of a large section of the Mala Mala Reserve.

I find it nostalgic to sign off on lions, particularly as they have been such a major factor in my life—and several times of equal consideration in what then seemed to be my impending death. Still, when the fire is low, and the razor blade of moon just a flicker, there's always the cry of the Old Africa, the call that so clearly says that man will never be completely dominant over the ancient but nubile black body of the lady who really controls my heart. The KiSwahili speakers understand the lion's long *UUUUnnnHHHH, Uhhh, Uhhh, Uhhh,* best, I think, interpreting the hollow, echoing challenge of *Simba* that rolls across the liquid darkness of rivers and the muted dun of plain from incredible miles as follows:

"Hi inchi ya nani?" translate the tribesmen with the suppression of a shudder. "Whose land is this?"

"Yangu, yangu, yangu."

"Mine, mine, mine."

Believe it, Charlie.

———————◆———————

The bold sagas of Pat James Byrne are fantastic reading. Getting mauled by a great predator, however, is necessarily ghastly. Only a madman would place romance and trauma on the same stalk. That age had diminished the lion in this story to a sad and desperate man-eater in no way lessens the pain of Vina Mbungla's wounds. Yet despite the horrors Elfas and Vina Mbungla suffered in that jungle hut, the story nonetheless embodies the jewel of the universe: that for all our bumbling and smallness, a person's regard for another can mean more than his or her very life.

The voice in our head tells us many things: "Elfas did what he was supposed to do." "He'd have been half a man if he'd acted differently." But a person who yells "I will save you" into the face of his own destruction, who beats the back of a savage lion with a wooden broomstick—this person hears only one voice. Where does that voice come from? Why does it yield such power and conviction? I don't know. I only know that it is the one thing mightier than our fight-or-flight response that lies in the basement of our psyches. This voice is deeper still. Without it, nothing human would be possible, least of all tying your spouse up in the rafters out of harm's way while you go it alone with a deranged and starving lion.

J.L.

Nightmare Hunt

Rollin Braden as told to Marguerite Reiss

My hunting buddy, Darrel Rosin, chided me as we pushed aside the high brush on the narrow path leading back to the cabin.

"Thought you told me these bears up here go after moose nose like kids after ice cream," Darrel kidded. "Here we've been on this moose hunt for two weeks and nary the sign of a bear. Just doesn't stack up."

Whether we had seen them or not, we were in bear country. It was the tag end of the moose season in southern Alaska, fifty miles south of Soldotna, two hundred miles south of Anchorage.

I was getting anxious about our lack of success as the end of our trip drew near. Finally, my dad, Wes, and my brother, Wayne, managed to get their moose on the same day, but neither Darrel nor I scored.

On one of the last days of our moose hunt, Darrel and I started off through the high willows that surrounded our camp. We had our minds set on adding two more moose carcasses to those already hanging in the tree near the cabin.

Darrel figured that he'd get his from a platform we had built twenty feet up in a tall spruce tree four years earlier. It was a terrific lookout, commanding a splendid view across the thick brush, spruce stands, and tundra bogs.

Darrel let it be known that he was going to get his moose if it took him all day—and it nearly did. At 5 P.M., I heard a shot from Darrel's Ruger 77.

"Got him!" I heard Darrel yell. "At one hundred yards."

It was a little after 7 P.M. when we finished dressing his kill and were starting back to the cabin to stow our meat ax, saw, and rope.

The spruce shadows were, for me, depressingly long. Darrel had gotten his moose, but I was still empty-handed. I was thinking of using up the last half hour or so of twilight to locate a bull that I knew had been with the rest of the bulls we'd taken.

If I couldn't get him tonight, I'd get him at first light tomorrow. Only one day of the season remained.

I stepped just a couple of feet away from Darrel and stopped, listening. Though I couldn't explain it, the silence cloaking the wilderness seemed somehow different. But then, the whole two weeks of September 1985 had been different.

I checked my compass and shoved it in a rear pocket of my hunting pants. I thought to myself that Dad and Wayne were just about finishing their spaghetti dinner a couple of miles down the road at the cabin of our friend, Lou Clarke. I also was thinking how spooky everything seemed out here in the deep twilight and vast wilderness. It was then that I heard a faint rustling in the brush a hundred feet or so away.

"It's your moose," Darrel called out. "Go get him, buster."

That rustling was almost a summons. That was my moose. I had to get him—now. Somehow I wanted to be alone when I got him.

"Go on ahead," I told Darrel. "I'm going back to meet him. What'll you bet he's a seventy-incher?"

"Shout 'whoopee' when you get him," Darrel hollered, waving me off and continuing toward the cabin. ✗

Now the adrenaline was flowing through me—but good. I was as anxious and fired up as I had been on previous hunting trips when I got my eight moose. Each year, it seemed, those moments before the kill got more and more tense and anxious. I cut back the way we had come, angling northward in the direction of the intermittent rustling. Everything seemed fine. I kept low, crouching, on the lookout for anything that moved, testing each step for noise before I shifted my entire weight, and listening for sounds up ahead.

Realizing that the bull might be closer to me than I'd figured earlier, I geared up mentally for sudden action at close range. Another deep and eerie silence settled, and quieting my anxious thoughts wasn't easy. A spine-tingling sensation swept over me—the feeling that whatever I had been watching for in the thick brush up ahead had been, or maybe was, watching me. I didn't dare move fast.

I was waiting for the rustling sound, picturing a hefty bull, a moose with the longed-for seventy-inch rack, a critter far bigger than Dad's or Wayne's or all the eight moose I had taken in other years.

Suddenly, in a sound that came to me like the crack of summer lightning, underbrush snapped a couple of hundred feet away. I stared in the direction of the noise and heard another branch crack, only this time it was much louder. Slowly, just forty feet ahead, I saw the brush beginning to part. My breath stopped in my throat and I gasped as the leaves split apart like a green stage curtain revealing two of the fastest, biggest brown bears I'd ever seen, charging right at me.

"My God!" I heard myself stammer.

In a flash, I took stock. I had a few seconds—no more—to shoot at the half-growling, half-grunting, charging beasts. One was barrelling half a length in front of the other. I yelled, but they kept right on coming—their ugly brown faces glistening in the twilight, the rolling fur on their backs undulating like waves on the ocean.

Their huge jaws were open, revealing rows of razor-sharp teeth plainly visible at 30 feet. Their big heads reared up when they saw me, their tongues hanging out. They neither hesitated nor slowed down. Now there was no time for fear or paralysis. Each bear must have weighed four or five hundred pounds. In that split second, they looked to me like monsters from outer space.

It is amazing how much agility comes with reflex in a life-or-death situation. I whirled to the right, hoping that my .338-caliber Ruger 77 would do the job.

I shot from the waist. The crack of my rifle seemed to reverberate for miles. I looked ahead. "My God," I thought, "nothing's changed." The bears were glaring, still charging toward me. I'm a crack shot but, this time, when it really mattered, I missed. Besides, when two are coming, which one do you aim for? The bullet hit a tree.

Now plainly visible were the ugly, yellow, razor spikes of teeth protruding from drooling jaws. I froze. Time seemed to stop, and I remember glancing at the beasts' claws for just a second. Before I could chamber another round, they'd be on me. I spun on my heels; now my back was to them and I was braced for their first blows. I dropped my rifle and threw my hands over my face, shielding my eyes. As I did this, the bears lunged. I felt a staggering blow against my back and then a force like a team of linebackers struck my shoulders, knocking me down. Sharp sticks cut my lips and weeds jammed in my mouth. My nose and forehead were wedged flat against the forest moss. Then, a ton of weight like the wheels of a car pinned down my back. I could hear strange, thick, guttural animal sounds and the sound of spasmodic breathing.

What I decided then was wrong—I know it now, but I wasn't thinking clearly at the time. I had been thrashing my arms and legs, but it suddenly occurred to me that my struggle was futile. "Why fight?" I asked myself. "You're dead already. Why resist?" At that moment, one of the bears started chewing my ear after knocking my cowboy hat off.

Something in me advised: "Play dead. Bears are supposed to get disinterested and leave. But you've got to lie perfectly still." Still? "Dear God, how?" a voice within me screamed. I jammed my thumbs down into the earth as the first of countless agonizing needles began piercing my buttocks and up and down my spine. Now, the slashing attack moved higher.

Horror swept me as I felt pressure like a foot, near my ear. Then the real agony—I felt one of the beasts yanking my head up to get a better grip on my neck. Stifling a scream, I ground my mouth into the ground.

The grating sound intensified. Instead of letting up, the bears began getting more ferocious. My entire body was being shoved and shaken with tremendous animal power. My knees were being stomped and ground down into the brush. One of the beasts was working on my back, the other on my skull. Then, they traded places. The sequence of events is hard to sort out, though. My mental pictures of the agony are mercifully blurred.

I fought to keep from moving or twitching. Something in me seemed to be ordering me to lie still, motionless, but my body rebelled and my left leg twitched sharply. Every time there was movement, it was followed by a burst of more needles of shooting pain. I had a mental image of one of the bears clamping its open jaws around the entire top of my head, attempting to crush in the bones, but not quite succeeding. I heard the animals panting in my ears. I figured that I was in the throes of death. Death from bleeding. Death from shock.

They chewed on my head and back for what seemed hours, or days. Then they stopped abruptly to rest. I sprawled absolutely motionless and silent, my heart thumping wildly. I could feel my pulse pounding in my wrists and temples.

"Lie still," I warned myself. "Don't move. You've lost a lot of blood. Try to run and they'll flatten you and finish the job. If you as much as twitch, you're done for."

I stiffened my knees to hold them firm, but the effort brought movement that instantly caught the bears' attention and brought both of them roaring to a standing position. Then they settled back and I could see them several yards away, their piglike eyes glaring at me.

Miraculously, I was still alive—but for how long? How many arteries and blood vessels can rupture before you bleed to death? How many slashes can you take and still remain perfectly motionless?

Somehow, it comforted me to think about what I had been told all my life: After they kill, bears will refuse to immediately devour a human meal. They have been known to gulp down a moose kill, but you can count on them moving off without completely devouring the remains of a man. Sometimes, they return to cover the meat with leaves and twigs, but they go away for days until decomposition progresses to a certain stage. Bears have been known to relish rancid meat. But a fresh kill? They usually walk off as if it were poison.

I'll never forget the wave of relief and thankfulness that swept over me when the creatures were no longer on my back, jabbing and pulling.

"Are they gone?" a voice inside me asked. "Look and see."

Saliva clogged my mouth and throat. Slowly, I turned my head to the left. My face was caked with blood-soaked dirt, so I wiped my eyes and tried to look into the distance. That was all those waiting bears needed. Roaring, they were back at me, pouncing with new ferocity. One of them clamped its fangs on my shoulder, sending sharp teeth deep into muscle as pain zigzagged down my side, down my leg, to my toes. Now they began in earnest to rip the flesh at the back of my skull.

Despite the intense pain, the only thing on my mind was my children.

"Dear God," I begged, "let me live. I want to see Max and Melinda again. God, let me live."

Things seemed to go blank for a moment and the scene wavered. Then, as if I were detached from the horror now enveloping me, a part of me began lecturing to the other part. I heard myself say, "Go limp.... Repeat over and over: I am still, still as death. I will let them chew. I will not move.... I will play dead ... play dead.... Let it happen.... Let them have me...."

"I can't," a part of me resisted.

"Yes, you can. Repeat: I will let them chew. I will not move. I will play dead." My inner voice seemed to be repeating the admonitions over and over.

I do not know how many minutes or seconds this eerie confab went on. I had long since lost track of how much time had passed. Tremors of pain were cutting into my chest now. A new and terrible fear seized me as the bears moved from my back to other parts of my body and alongside my lungs.

Then, in one moment, all of life seemed to ebb and stand still. Gone was the slurping, pulling, grunting, crunching, licking. Silence. Dead silence. "How," I wondered, "can something so huge move off so fast and so silently?"

But I knew they were nearby, sitting only yards away, their eyes watching for the slightest movement, their ears tensed for the slightest sound from my body. I forced myself not to look, not to raise my head, not to move so much as a finger or an eyelash. Now, all was deep, agonizing silence. Nothing moved. From my limbs, neck, and face, blood seeped silently into the dirt. My body seemed frozen, glued down, a part of the earth. Motionless, I listened. Now there was no rustling, no footsteps, no dry twigs breaking.

"Dear God," I thought, "do I dare raise my head? Will they come at me again?"

I kept my eyes closed tight and a kind of peace filtered through the pain. I saw the little church that I attended in Soldotna. I saw my dad and mom. I saw my sister JoAnn and my brothers. I was with them and suddenly, somehow, I got the courage to lift my head just a little bit so I could look around.

The bears were gone. But how far? Were they lurking just behind that clump of spruce trees, ready to charge again? I had no idea where the bears were, but I told myself that, if they came back, I'd let them finish me off and end my suffering. I didn't want any more of that awful pain. But they weren't around, and somehow I had to find the strength to get away.

"Try getting up," I told myself. "See if you can stand without falling." Was I brain-damaged in the attack? I had to be able to think. If a lot of my brain was gone, would I be rational? Could I trust my thinking?

Fighting back the pain, I somehow was able to get on my feet. I realized then that my legs hadn't been broken. I lifted my hands to feel my head. My hand slid under my scalp as under a hat. I took my binoculars off over my head, unbuttoned my wool shirt with one hand, and slipped down my suspenders to strip off my shirt. There was no way I could let go of my head and remove my shirt without the loosened skin sliding out of place.

"I've got to get out of here fast," I kept thinking, "but which way?" New blood poured down my cheeks, soaking my pants and shirt.

Despite all this, I felt no revulsion, just an aching hope that somehow I might get my shirt tied around my head to hold everything in place until I could get help. I could see partially, but every movement I made seemed to increase the bleeding and to bring on greater weakness.

"Dear Lord," I prayed, "all the trees look the same. Show me which way to go. Help me to choose the right direction."

"Maybe," I thought, "the bears are still lurking around."

"Help me," I muttered aloud. "Help me." Then I yelled, "Darrel! Darrel! Help."

I started to run. To this day I don't know how, but I pushed the tall grass aside, stumbling, screaming. "Darrel! Help!"

Darrel heard my yelling. He cut back into the woods in the direction of my voice and then stopped dead in his tracks.

"Dear God!" he said as he saw me. "Oh, my God!"

I thought he was going to faint, but he helped me back to the cabin. Dad and Wayne were there when we arrived.

Someone gave me a mirror. I couldn't believe that the awfully mangled creature I saw was me. The entire back of my head, ear to ear, had been opened and lifted. The scalp was falling to the front like a slipped wig. A piece of scalp was missing. Punctures in my shoulder were so deep that I thought my lungs might be pierced. My back and legs were covered with gashes and bites. The bears' teeth had punctured through more than three inches of buttocks flesh. My head had been chewed badly. Sticks, grass, dirt, and bear saliva were in the wounds. My favorite watch, the one I liked because it was thin and easy on the hunt, was crunched through the dial. It had stopped at exactly 7:33 P.M.

Working swiftly, Darrel made a tourniquet out of a towel and tightened it around my head. Dad, meanwhile, cleaned the blood from my face and body.

The guys flung a mattress onto the trailer and I climbed in. The trailer was hooked into our four-wheeler. By now, the pain was beginning to break through my consciousness as the protecting shock wore away.

Wayne was driving, and he frantically spun the wheels in his haste to get us out of the cabin and through the woods to our pickup truck parked six miles away. Once we got to the truck, we would drive sixty miles to Soldotna, where there would be a doctor and a plane to take me to Providence Hospital in Anchorage, two hundred miles away.

The white bath towel that the guys had given me had turned bright red. The pain in one of my buttocks was so great that I shifted my body in the trailer. It was too much effort to reach into my wool pants pocket to see what was jabbing me whenever we hit a bump. (I later found out that it was a chewing tobacco can.)

Conversation was sparse as we drove to the pickup truck. Darrel seemed to be feeling guilty about having not responded when he heard my shout and the shot I fired. But, at the time, Darrel thought that I had gotten my moose and was yelling "whoopee."

"I was so happy for you," he said. "I threw my hat in the air and hollered, 'Yiii-eee! Another moose bit the dust.' If only I had known."

What none of us knew was that more surprises were still in store. We got to the pickup only to find that we had to change a flat tire. Our troubles continued at the airline counter in Soldotna. There were no planes in the airport, so one was ordered to be flown out of Anchorage.

I arrived in the emergency room of Providence Hospital at 3 A.M. My physician, Dr. Jim Scully of Anchorage, spent five hours applying two hundred stitches and flushing and picking pine needles from my skull.

———◆———

"My breath stopped in my throat and I gasped as the leaves split apart like a green stage curtain revealing two of the fastest, biggest brown bears I'd ever seen, charging right at me."

Rollin Braden was about to become both actor and audience of the Brown Bear Horror Show. Because he survived, it's hard to say that Rollin was reading off the wrong script; yet, as the following commentary insists, he was probably wrong to play dead. But who can blame him for doing so, and who can match his resolve in remaining limp as the great bears played tag-team with his head?

Every outdoorsman is thankful that this kind of attack is uncommon. It can possibly be understood only in the context of general information known and verified by experts.

Only the rare North American will ever face the possibility of attack by a Bengal tiger or a rogue elephant; most wilderness travelers, however, have at least seen a bear in the wild. It's worth reviewing the analysis of Mike Cramond, who has done extensive research on the nature of bear attacks:

> A rather surprising statistic shows that by overwhelming majority, those who fought or used some sort of physical defense survived bear attacks. Of the eighty-two who chose to fight, seventy-three survived. Of those who were known to have lain still or feigned dead, fourteen survived and three died. Of those who ran, four were killed and eighteen lived. . . .

> Campers are commonly advised to first shuck and drop any pack, whether it contains food or not, and thus allow the dropped article to distract the animal's attention. It is also recommended that you discard items of food or clothing while retreating. However, such an approved method does not assure even a momentary delay of the actual charge of a bear. . . .

> Any person—trapper, seasoned hunter, bushman, park, forest, or game warden or experienced scientist—who has closely studied any or all bear species readily draws the conclusion: all bears are to be considered dangerous and likely to attack with or without provocation. . . .

> Although it is common legend that black bears are sneaky and will attack from behind, the attack by grizzlies has been proven in several cases to be by ambush. This means that the probability of sudden, unexpected attack from cover is a possibility—however remote—anywhere in the wild. . . .

J.L.

The Killer Leopard of Manyara

Frank C. Hibben

The mouth was open, the lips were wrinkled back. Two eyes were streaks of green-yellow light.

The cat head lunged forward. The open teeth were a blur of motion. The impact knocked the gun from David's hands. There was a paralyzing blow on his throat. He was thrown and pinned like a wrestler in a match for death.

It was no accident that the leopard stood over the body of David Ommanney. David himself could have foretold that this would happen. For one thing, there were the bad omens; and, for another, there were the leopard themselves. Only that morning he had told his client, Baron von Boeselager, that the African leopard is the most dangerous animal in existence. "For its size and weight," David had pronounced solemnly, "the leopard is the most ferocious game on four legs. When a leopard is wounded, he *always* charges. And when he charges, he usually gets there with his teeth."

It was not that Baron von Boeselager did not believe David. Actually, the Baron had hunted twice in Africa before, and had shot all of the African Big Five, the animals that bite back. Even though the leopard is usually mentioned last in the list of the dangerous five, he is considered by many white hunters to be the most deadly of the whole quintet. Both the Baron and David Ommanney had heard, just before they started on this trip, that Eric Rundgren of the safari firm of Ker and Downey had been mauled by a leopard in the Narok district in southwestern Kenya. Dave Lunan, another white hunter, had also been badly chewed by a leopard near Lake Manyara, in northern Tanganyika, only a short time before.

And yet at the close of January, 1959, Baron von Boeselager and his white hunter, David Ommanney, had set up camp in the very country where Lunan had almost met his death. The reason was simple. The Baron wanted a male leopard at least two and a half meters in length. Dangerous or not, some of the best leopard in all of East Africa are to be found in the Lake Manyara district. So David directed the safari boys to set up the camp on the flat plain two or three miles back from the edge of Lake Manyara itself. The country is level with scattered palm trees. Game is fairly abundant. There are many Grant's gazelle, impala, and wart hogs. Around the salt pans of Lake Manyara a herd of some five hundred buffalo habitually feed. Perhaps because the smaller varieties of game are abundant, the plain around the lake is crawling with leopard. For some reason, the Manyara leopard are more aggressive than leopard elsewhere. In the last ten years, two fatal leopard attacks and a dozen maulings have occurred in the Manyara district.

David Ommanney is one of the youngest full-fledged white hunters in East Africa. Nonetheless, he felt supremely confident as he directed the safari boys to set up camp and sent the trackers out to look for leopard sign. David was born in India in 1928, and lived most of his life at Nanyuki, on the slopes of Mount Kenya in Africa. He had been hunting leopard, and every other kind of game for that matter, since he was old enough to lift the butt of a rifle. David had dealt with the forest leopard on his native Mount Kenya, and had collected on safari dozens of the beautiful spotted cats in the brush country and grasslands of both Kenya and Tanganyika. By the time he was twenty, David had personally accounted for over twenty-five leopard.

It was an old story to David as he directed the Baron to shoot some small game for leopard bait. The first evening, on January 20, the trackers brought in the information that at least four leopard were working within a mile of camp, and were watering some distance back from the edge of the lake. The next morning, the Baron shot two wart hogs, a Grant's gazelle, and an impala. With the cunning born of long experience, Ommanney directed his first gun bearer Salim, and his second gun bearer, Mutia, to drag these baits, one at a time, through the grass and palmettos where the leopard would pass. Then, as each leopard moved down to drink after dark, he would smell the drag and go straight to the bait. Each carcass was placed high in a tree.

That very first day, the stage was set for tragedy. Baron von Boeselager shot a hyena. Perhaps the Baron did not know that hyenas are considered very bad luck. Most of the Masai tribe (and there were several Masai among David's safari boys) regard the hyena as bad because the animal is full of evil human spirits. When a Masai dies, his relatives never bury the body. They simply place the dead on the ground outside the village. In the evening, the ever-present hyenas eat every scrap of the human body, then crack the bones and eat those too. Hyenas often do not wait for native villagers to expose bodies, but will attack a sleeping man and bite off his arm or his face in a single snap. To the Masai, the hyena is a powerful animal, full of the evil of death.

The safari boys murmured among themselves, and rolled

their eyes at the ground, when the Baron shot the hyena. None of them would touch the dead animal. When the Baron wanted the animal skinned, and its head fixed for his trophy collection, not one of the skinners drew out his knife or made a move to save the carcass.

In the several days that followed, the incident of the hyena was almost forgotten, except by the most superstitious. During that time, the party found several leopard. Each of the leopard came to a bait which had been hung in one of the thorn trees on the plain. In two instances, the trackers could tell by the small size of the spoor that the leopard were but half-grown cats, not worthy of further attention. Three of the leopard, however, which had been to feed on the baits provided for them, were apparently large animals.

On each of three evenings, David and the Baron squatted in the high grass near one of these trees. At the first bait, they ascertained, by looking with binoculars at the carcass in the tree, that a leopard had appropriated the meat and was feeding upon it. From the amount of flesh eaten, they judged that the leopard was a large one, probably a male. They did not try to go near the tree from which the bait hung to get a closer look at the tracks. Such a rash action would either drive the leopard away, or, worse, provoke him into charging.

When leopard appropriate a kill, they feed upon it, and then lie up nearby, so as to keep an eye on the remains. If they kill the animal themselves, they usually haul the carcass into a tree for safe keeping. If the wily human places a Grant's gazelle or an impala in a tree, therefore, it seems very natural to a leopard. The leopard feeds by night on his kill. He usually comes in the evening, jumps into the tree, and fills his belly. After that, he will lie in some place of concealment near the tree, to guard the remains of the meat against would-be predators in the form of other leopard, hyenas, or birds of prey.

When David and the Baron slipped up to examine a leopard bait, they did so downwind, stealthily. They squatted in the high grass among the palmettos with only the tops of their heads showing. They made no unnecessary movement. The eyesight of a leopard is extremely keen. In whispered tones, Ommanney directed the Baron as to what to do. As the Baron had shot leopard before, he was steady, and the hunting went well.

But Baron von Boeselager was particular. The first leopard which they saw was a large male, better than seven feet in length. The animal appeared suddenly out of the grass. As the leopard jumped up into the thorn tree, the last slanting rays of the sun lighted up the orange-yellow body marked with beautiful black rosettes. This was a trophy of which any sportsman would have been proud.

The leopard was hungry. He looked around only once, and then lay at full length on a large limb and began to feed. David had laid his hand upon the Baron's elbow, so that there would be no movement which the leopard might see. When the cat began to eat, gulping down the rotten meat in great chunks, David signaled the Baron to raise his gun and fire. The Baron shook his head. "Two and a half meters," the Baron said firmly. Just behind Ommanney and the Baron, Salim, the gun bearer, swore a Moslem oath. The curse of Allah be upon this European. The misfortune of the hyena would overcome them all. Here was a fair shot in good light—and the leopard was a beauty.

But the Baron was determined to have a big leopard or none at all. On three successive evenings, the Baron shook his head firmly at three successive leopard. David himself was becoming irritated. For one thing, it was no small feat to attract five leopard in as many days. Not only had the leopard been induced to take the baits of gazelle and wart hog, but each bait had been placed just right.

Each leopard had fed for two or three nights so that the hunters had had a chance to look him over. Ommanney had led the Baron through the high grass in just the right way, so that the leopards would not be alarmed. Any one of the first

five leopard they could have shot with ease; but still the
Baron shook his head.

Perhaps it was the Baron's stubbornness; perhaps it was the
evil human spirit of the hyena, as Salim said. The sixth leopard was the one.

David, with some show of justifiable irritation, had directed the Baron rather curtly to get another wart hog, which
they would hang near a dry wash or donga some two miles
from camp. There were leopard tracks in the sand of this
wash. Two or three cats apparently used the donga as a high-
way going to and from water. The wart hog was appropriately
placed in a thorn tree.

The next morning, as David swung the safari car within two
or three hundred yards of the thorn tree, he could see that a
leopard had taken the bait. The wart hog had been a big boar,
yet almost all the carcass of the hog was gone. Only the head
and one shoulder remained. These grisly fragments, hanging
by remnants of skin, had been hoisted higher in the tree, and
now hung in the fork of a branch. The rope by which Salim
had tied the wart hog carcass had been bitten through, as if it
had been string. Only a very large leopard could do this. Perhaps this one would be big enough to satisfy the Baron.

It was uncertain whether the leopard would come back at
all. He had fed heavily that first night. Also, there was little
left for another meal—even for a hungry leopard. But it was a
chance. So David and the Baron squatted behind a group of
palmettos some fifty yards from the thorn tree on the edge of
the wash. Salim lay on his elbow behind them. As usual,
Salim shook his head and muttered under his breath. The
omens were bad. As the sun sank lower, a flight of pink
flamingos flew into the lake from behind: a very bad sign. A
hornbill stalked up and down a branch at the top of the thorn
tree. The hornbill squawked through his ridiculous overgrown beak, and to Salim the cries sounded like *"mbaya,
mbaya."* This means, in Swahili, "bad, bad."

It was bad, too, when the sun lowered and the leopard did not appear. The last rays slanted over the escarpment beyond Lake Manyara. As though this were a signal, there was a rasping growl from the grass.

They saw the leopard at the edge of the donga. The end of his tail twitched back and forth in little jerks. The leopard was looking straight at them.

"He'll go eight feet, maybe more," David hissed into the Baron's ear.

The Baron was already raising his gun. He carried a European-made over-and-under effect, with an 8.64 rifle barrel mounted above a 16 gauge shotgun. This was not an easy shot. The leopard they had seen before were broadside, and in plain sight in a tree. This leopard was facing the hunters and looking straight at them. Any second the cat would whirl and go. The leopard's chest was a target the size of two human hands.

The Baron sighted quickly and fired. The solid ball struck too far to the right. Ommanney could see the spurt of fur as the bullet raked along the leopard's ribs. The leopard jerked sideways, and leaped into the air. The squalling scream that came from between the wet teeth was a mixture of pain and rage. In an arching bound, the leopard jumped sideways into the waist-high grass. Frantically, Ommanney raised his .470 double rifle and fired. The bullet was too late. It nicked the hind paw of the leopard as he sailed into the grass.

Just as the leopard leaped, he turned in mid-air. He turned toward the three men. He had been looking at the humans before the shots. Now he was coming at them through the grass.

Ommanney grabbed the Baron by one arm. They ran sideways a few yards to where a termite hill rose out of the grass. Around the termite hill, the busy little insects had cut down the vegetation for several yards. As Ommanney and the Baron scrambled up the rough knobs of the termite mound, a cobra uncoiled and slid into one of the passageways. The Baron flinched to one side. Ommanney jerked him higher on the bare dirt. Cobras usually run from humans; wounded leopard never do.

From the elevation of the termite hill, the hunters could look down into the grass. There was no sight or sound. Over across the plain of Manyara, the three rocky hills known as the pyramids were lighted by the evening sun. A lion roared in the distance down by the lake. The grass around the termite hill was empty of life.

Salim offered David the double-barreled 12 gauge shotgun which he carried as an extra. A shotgun is standard armament on a leopard hunt. At close range the shotgun is more lethal than a rifle. Ommanney snapped open the weapon, and checked the two shells of buckshot in the breach. He directed the Baron to stay on top of the termite hill and have his rifle ready. Ommanney stepped down and into the fringe of thick grass to meet the leopard. With Salim at his heels, he moved slowly toward the edge of the donga and the tree where the remnants of the wart hog still hung. There was no noise or movement to show that any animal was within a mile of this quiet spot.

Perhaps ten yards from the place where the leopard had stood, David hesitated. Here there were low-growing palmettos mixed in the high grass. The leopard might attack from only a few feet away. He would need a second's warning to catch the charging animal on the end of his gun barrel.

David raised the shotgun and fired one barrel at the palmettos. He could still see nothing, but he listened carefully, expecting the leopard to growl at the shot and reveal his position. There was no sound. David reloaded and walked slowly forward. Again he raised the shotgun and fired, aiming at the exact spot where the leopard had disappeared. He waited tensely. Nothing. Even the birds had stopped their evening chirping.

He reloaded the empty barrel of the shotgun. Perhaps the Baron's shot had done its work after all. Ommanney stepped forward. He stood in the very grass where the leopard had jumped. With Salim peering over his shoulder, David swung slowly around. The leopard had gone.

A palmetto rustled. There was no wind. Fifteen feet away a yellow blur appeared. The thing was six feet in the air. Blindly David fired both barrels. He saw white teeth in front of his face. A paralyzing blow struck his throat. His gun flew end over end. He fell backward. Salim behind him was knocked down.

The leopard stood over him. When David looked up, he saw a white throat from beneath. Bloody saliva dripped down over the open jaws. The leopard turned to growl at Salim. The cat's face bent downwards. David saw the open mouth lunge at his throat. Instinctively, he threw up his left arm. He tried to twist sideways. The weight of the leopard lay upon him. "Must keep those teeth from my throat," he thought. The fangs closed on his shoulder as he twisted. At the first bite, his leather jacket was shredded. Muscle and bone crunched between the teeth. The leopard growled deep in his chest. The teeth shifted their grip lower, to try again for the throat. Again David twisted frantically. The teeth sank in near his elbow. David could hear tendons and muscles breaking away.

Salim sprawled on the ground. The double rifle had been knocked from his hands. The leopard lay over bwana David. As the leopard lunged forward for the kill, Salim drew his knife—the curved knife that all Mohammedans wear. With it, Salim cut the throats of animals so that orthodox Mohammedans could eat the meat.

With the knife held high, Salim took one running step. He launched himself into the air in a flying tackle. As he struck the leopard on the back, he lunged downward with his knife. He felt the blade go through skin and meat.

The leopard squawked in pain. He turned. Raking talons

curved from the side. Salim rolled clear over the leopard. He still held the knife. The leopard stood there. He swung his head, first at the unconscious Ommanney, then at Salim. Which of the two men would he kill first? With a low growl, the leopard turned and jumped into the grass.

Salim stooped over bwana David. Ommanney's eyes flickered. He raised his head weakly. Salim helped him to his knees. Blood was pumping in spurts from the severed arteries in his upper arm. Weakly, he tried to hold the blood back with his right hand. The muscles and tendons of his left arm were hanging in shreds. If he had not worn a leather jacket, his arm would have been gone entirely.

Baron von Boeselager and Salim supported David on either side. Ommanney's strength was failing rapidly, as blood poured down his left hand in a flood. By the time they reached the safari car, the pyramid mountains and the thorn trees were swimming before him. At camp, the Baron snatched rolls of bandage from the first-aid kit, and with them he staunched the flow of blood. The native driver was already in the seat of the safari car. Arusha and the hospital were seventy-five miles away.

When David was on his way to help in the safari car, the faithful Salim began to wonder. Had his knife found its way between the leopard's ribs? Was the leopard dead, back there in the grass? It is the code of the hunters that a wounded and dangerous animal may not be left alone; otherwise, the next person to pass that way will surely be killed.

Salim went to the edge of the camp, where the safari boys were huddled together. They talked in low voices about the leopard which had nearly killed bwana David. Salim called to Mutia, the second gun bearer. He thrust a .30-06 rifle into Mutia's unwilling hands. Then, having loaded Ommanney's .470 double rifle, he motioned Mutia to follow.

Twilight was beginning to darken the Manyara Valley when Salim and Mutia again approached the bait tree and the edge of the donga. There was the place in the matted grass where bwana Ommanney had fallen. There, too, was the pool of blood, already growing dark and sticky. Just beyond was the place where Salim himself had rolled, after he had knifed the leopard. And just there, in the high grass, was where the leopard had gone.

Salim took a step. The grass rustled. The leopard was already in the air. Salim half raised the gun. One barrel went off. The bullet plowed into the ground. The leopard caught him full in the face. One tooth ripped through his eye. As Salim fell over backward, raking claws tore at his belly and his thigh.

Mutia threw up his rifle and fired blindly. The leopard's tail was cut by the bullet. The leopard screeched wildly. The cat turned. Darting his head downward, he bit Salim through the shoulder. Salim could feel the teeth crunch through the bone. Then he lost consciousness.

Mutia managed to get another shell into the chamber of the .30-06. Again he shot. The leopard, writhing on top of Salim, was only feet away. The shot went wild. At the noise, the leopard stood up. He growled. Then he turned and leaped into the high grass. Half of the leopard's tail lay across Salim's knees.

Just after dark, Baron von Boeselager used the rest of the bandages from the first-aid kit to tie up Salim's thigh and shoulder. The teeth of the leopard had missed the jugular vein by a fraction of an inch. Salim's eye was gouged away. The Baron had the safari boys put the unconscious Salim on a mattress in the back of the truck. He drove the truck himself into Arusha. The hospital there received the second victim of the Manyara leopard a scant two hours after the first. From Mutia's story, they learned that the leopard still was not dead.

That night, over the telephone wires, went the story from Arusha to Nairobi: "A killer leopard is in the Manyara country. A safari is leaderless. We need help."

Theo Potgieter, a white hunter for the firm of Selby and Holmberg, was the only qualified hunter in Nairobi, as most white hunters were on safari. Potgieter, just in from his last hunting trip, answered the emergency.

It was Friday when the Manyara leopard had attacked David Ommanney and almost killed the brave Salim. It was Sunday before Potgieter could find his own gun bearer and drive the 150 odd miles from Nairobi to Arusha. It was Sunday afternoon, January 26, when Theo Potgieter reached the disorganized camp on the Manyara plain. That same afternoon, with Mutia and Baron von Boeselager, Theo went after the leopard.

Mutia still carried Ommanney's .30-06, but Mutia stayed well behind. From a safe distance, he pointed out the trampled grass where the leopard had attacked Salim. Potgieter found the spot. The matted ground was rusty with dried blood. Jackals had carried off the leopard's tail. Of the tailless leopard himself, there was no sign.

Theo directed the Baron to take his station on the termite hill. With the double-barreled shotgun at eye level, and the safety off, Potgieter walked slowly through the high grass. David had described to him, from his hospital bed, the charge of the leopard. "It was fast as light," David had said. "He was in the air before my face when I saw him."

Theo moved slowly, the shotgun ever before him. He kicked at the palmettos around the place where Ommanney and Salim had met the leopard. There was no sound. The leopard had gone. But just to make sure, Theo made a wider circle. He beat up and down the high grass on the edge of the donga for a hundred yards. He circled beyond the bait tree, back and forth. The grass was undisturbed. The wounded leopard had gone off and died.

Potgieter moved back towards the termite mound where the Baron waited tensely. Again the sun was lowering beyond the escarpment. A palmetto leaf rustled to Potgieter's left. He jerked around. The leopard was already in the air. Potgieter swung the gun. The first barrel burned fur on the leopard's neck. Frantically he pulled the second barrel. The buckshot tore into the leopard's shoulder. The momentum of the leopard's leap struck against Potgieter's chest. The gun flew from his hands. He rolled away. The leopard stood there. His left paw hung limp. The leopard was far from dead. His ears were laid back. He wrinkled his lips. On three legs he lunged forward.

Theo threw up his arm before his face. In a second, the leopard would be at his throat.

A shot blasted out. Potgieter did not feel the tearing teeth. He raised his head. Three feet from him, the leopard twitched on the matted grass. The bloody stump of a tail thrashed back and forth in death. The Baron's shot had caught the killer leopard in the neck.

"Yes," said David Ommanney when he left the hospital with his left arm in a cast, "there are a lot of dangerous animals in Africa, but for my money, the leopard is the fastest and the worst. And," he added slowly, "I'm never going to allow a client to kill another hyena."

———————◆———————

Lost eyes, torn limbs . . . if I've learned something from compiling this collection it's that a wounded leopard is a full-scale disaster. How could David Ommanney have possibly avoided setting this disaster in motion?

Trying to second-guess any kind of adventure calamity can be dangerous if we're trying to place blame, but not if we're trying to realize something. And, when reading this piece, I realized that the terrible lessons learned from the recent Mt. Everest tragedy (fourteen people died) apply directly to the misfortunes surrounding the killer leopard of Manyara.

The Everest tragedy involved paying customers and professional guides. Experience and judgment are what the clients paid for but did not receive. The problem started when the aspirations of the clients were put above the instincts and rules of the guides. Because the clients had paid to take a shot at the top of the world, the guides were all but expected to do everything except pull the clients to the summit. But much like the leopard in our story, Everest is unforgiving when things turn bad. In the Everest tragedy, the guides knew that if a summit party didn't head down by one o'clock, climbers would risk being caught on the mountain in bad weather. In deference to their client's aspirations, who were then so very close to the top, the guides broke their own rules and pushed the retreat time from one, to two, and finally to three o'clock. A storm moved in, and the rest is history.

David Ommanney knew that just before he and the Baron started on their safari, another hunter had been badly chewed by a leopard near Lake Manyara. Yet Baron von Boeselager and David Ommanney set up camp in the very country where the hunter had almost died. Why? The Baron wanted to shoot a male leopard at least two and a half meters in length. Then the Baron shoots a hyena and hauls bad luck into the equation.

"The first leopard which they saw was a large male, better than seven feet in length. The animal appeared suddenly out of the grass . . . a trophy of which any sportsman would have been proud." But the Baron shook his head. "Two and a half meters," the Baron said firmly.

Salim, the gun bearer, swore a Moslem oath. "The curse of Allah be upon this European."

The curse seemed to be on David Ommanney, however, because like the guides on Everest, the client was now leading the guide. Yes, the guide must make every effort for the trophy, or the summit, but when instincts say that the aspirations are unrealistic and the consequences grim or even fatal, and said instincts are waived in favor of the summit or the leopard, both the climber and the hunter are no longer playing the game on their terms. And, as we've already seen, playing on a leopard's terms is a deadly affair.

J.L.

———————◆———————

Attacked by a Killer Shark!

Rodney Fox

Kay looked miserable standing there as I said goodby at 6:30 that Sunday morning in December 1963. She was expecting our first child, and the doctor had told her firmly: don't go.

I wish now that the doctor's advice had applied to me as well. Two hours later, however, found me standing on the cliff at Aldinga Beach, 34 miles south of our home in Adelaide, South Australia. Given my early start, I had time to study carefully the dark patterns of bottom growth on the coral reef that shelves to seaward under the incoming blue-green swells.

Aldinga reef is a teeming sea jungle and happy hunting ground for underwater spearfishermen like myself. Forty of us were waiting for the referee's nine-o'clock whistle to announce that the annual South Australian Skin-Diving and Spearfishing Championship competition had begun. Each of us would have five hours to bring in to the judges the biggest bag, reckoned both by total weight and by number of different species of fish.

My own chances looked good. I had taken the 1961–62 championship and had been runner-up the following season. I had promised Kay that this would be my last competition. I meant to clinch the title and retire a winner, diving thenceforth only for fun, when Kay and I both might want to. I was 23 and, after months of training, at the peak of form. We were "free divers," using only wet suits, fins, face masks, snorkels, weigh belts and spearfishing guns. No SCUBA tanks allowed. I had trained myself to dive safely to 100 feet and to hold my breath for more than a minute without discomfort. At the nine-o'clock whistle blast we waded into the surf.

By way of a light line tied to our lead weight-belts, each man towed behind him a buoyant, hollow fish float. We would load our fish into these floats immediately after spearing them. This would minimize the amount of fresh blood released in the water. Blood might attract from out beyond the reef the big hunting fish—the always ravenous and lethal predatory sharks that prowl the deeper water off the South Australian coast. Lesser sharks—like the bronze whaler and gray nurse—are familiar to skin divers and have not proved aggressive. Fortunately the dread white hunter, or "white death" sharks, caught by professional fishermen in the open ocean, are rarely encountered by skin divers. But as a precaution two high-powered patrol boats crisscrossed our hunting area, keeping a wary lookout.

The weather was bright and hot. An offshore breeze flattened the green wave tops, but it roiled the water on the reef. Visibility under the surface would be poor, making it difficult for us to zero in on potential game. In murky water a diver often gets too close to a fish before he realizes that it's there; thus he scares it away before he can get set for a clean shot.

By 12:30, when I towed to shore a heavy catch of parrot

fish, snapper, snook, boarfish, and magpie perch, I could see from the other piles that I was well up in the competition. I had 60 pounds of fish on shore, comprising 14 species. It was now 12:35, and the contest closed at two. As fish naturally grew scarcer in the inshore areas I had ranged out to three quarters of a mile for bigger and better game. On my last swim-in from the "drop off" section of the reef, where it plunges from 25-foot to 60-foot depth, I had spotted quite a few large fish near a big, triangular-shaped rock that I felt sure I could find again.

Two of these fish were dusky morwongs—or "strongfish," as Australian skin divers usually call them. Either of these would be large enough to tip the scales in my favor; then one more fish of another variety would sew things up for me. I swam out to the spot I'd picked, then rested face down, breathing through my snorkel as I studied through my face glass the best approach to the two fish sheltering behind the rock. After several deep breaths I held one, swallowed to lock it in, up-ended and dived.

Swimming down and forward, so as not to spook them, I rounded the large rock and thrilled to see my quarry. Not 30 feet away the larger dusky morwong, a beauty of at least 20 pounds, was browsing in a clump of brown weed.

I glided forward, hoping for a close-in shot. I stretched both hands out in front of me, my left for balance, my right holding the gun, which was loaded with a stainless-steel shaft and barb. I drifted easily over the short weed and should have lined up for a perfect head-and-gill shot, but . . .

How can I describe the sudden silence? It was a perceptible *hush,* even in that quiet world, a motionlessness that was somehow communicable deep below the surface of the sea. Then something huge hit me with tremendous force on my left side, knocking my spear gun violently from my hand and ripping away my face mask. Heaved through the water at wild speed, I could see nothing in the blur.

I felt a bewildering sensation of nausea. The pressure on my back and chest was immense. A queer "cushiony" feeling ran down my right side, as if my insides on my left were being squeezed over to my right side.

The pressure on my body was choking me. Stunned senseless, I had no idea what was happening. I tried to shake myself loose but found that my body was clamped as if in a vise. With awful revulsion my mind came into focus, and I realized my predicament: *a shark had me in his jaws.*

I could not see the creature, but it had to be a huge one. Its teeth had closed around my chest and back, with my left shoulder forced into its throat. I was being thrust face down ahead of it as we raced through the water.

Although dazed with the horror, I felt no pain. In fact, there was no sharp feeling at all except for the crushing pressure on my back and chest. I stretched my arms out behind and groped for the monster's head, hoping to gouge its eyes.

Suddenly, miraculously, the pressure was gone from my chest. The creature had relaxed its jaws. I thrust backward to push myself away—but my right arm went straight into the shark's mouth.

Now I felt pain such as I had never imagined. Blinding bursts of agony made every part of my body scream in torment. As I wrenched my arm loose from the shark's jagged teeth, all-encompassing waves of pain swept through me. But I had succeeded in freeing myself.

I thrashed and kicked my way to the surface, thudding repeatedly into the shark's body. Finally my head pushed above water and I gulped great gasps of air. I knew the shark would come up for me. A fin brushed my flippers and then my knees suddenly touched its rough side. I grabbed with both arms, wrapping my legs and arms around the monster, hoping wildly that this maneuver would keep me out of his jaws. Somehow I gulped a great breath.

We went down again, so deep that I scraped the rocks on the bottom. Now I was shaken violently from side to side. I pushed away with all my remaining strength. I had to get back to the surface.

Once again I could breathe. But all around, the water was crimson with blood—my blood. The shark breached the surface a few feet away and turned over on its side. Its hideous body resembled a great rolling tree trunk, rust-colored, with huge pectoral fins. The great conical head belonged unmistakably to a white hunter. Here was the white-death itself!

It began moving toward me. Indescribable terror surged through my body. This fearful monster, this scavenger of the sea, was my master. I was alone in its domain; here the shark made the rules. I was no longer an Adelaide insurance salesman, rather a maimed and squirming meal, to be forgotten even before it was digested.

I knew the shark was attacking again and that I would die in agony when it struck. I could only wait. I breathed a hurried little prayer for Kay and the baby.

Then, in awe and disbelief, I saw the creature veer away just before it reached me, the slanted dorsal fin curving off just above the surface. The monster flashed to the buoy and swallowed it whole. The attached rope must have missed the severing teeth and lodged in the toothless, hinge section at the back of the jaw. The slack line tightened at my belt and I was wrenched forward and under the water again, dragged at shocking speed directly out to open sea. I tried to release my weight-belt to which the line was attached, but my arms would not obey. We were moving like a torpedo now and had traveled to a depth of 30 or 40 feet. My left hand continued fumbling helplessly at the release catch. Normally I use my right hand for everything. Now my right hand was free and empty, yet I instinctively used my left hand to claw at the belt. Although I had no conscious realization of my injuries, there must have been some subconscious knowledge that four tendons had been cut, rendering the fingers on my right hand useless. My left arm was also in a bad way, slashed deeply beneath the triceps muscle.

Again, my hand slid down by my belly-button to flick the quick-release—but there was no buckle. With the tow of the shark's great force pulling at the center of my body, my progress was erratic, a surging, swirling, spinning nightmare as I groped with my left hand to my right side, running fingers along the belt, groping for the quick-release. The little air I had gulped down before being hauled back under was now exhausted. My mind became fuzzier every second. I realized that the belt must have slipped around my waist as the shark hauled me into the deep. I no longer had the air nor the strength to stretch my arm around my back in a final search for the buckle. Now, I was finished. I had done what I could.

Then a miracle occurred: right alongside my belt the rope snapped and I was free once more. Normally the rope would have taken more strain, but apparently when the shark had bitten me around the chest he had partly cut through the rope, leaving only a few strands intact. I kicked frantically up toward the light. They tell me that all I could scream when my head reached the surface was: "Shark! . . . Shark!" It was enough.

Now there were voices, familiar noises, then the boatful of friends that I'd been praying would come. I gave up trying to move and relied on them. I couldn't even offer my arms, they were so torn. They rolled me into the boat and I collapsed on the seat. They elevated my legs and raced for shore. In this new world of people, somebody kept saying, "Hang on, mate, it's over. Hang on." I think without that voice urging me on I would have died. On the way in, the patrol boat picked up a few more divers.

The men in the boat were horrified at the extent of my injuries. Bruce Farley was one fellow they had picked up on the way in; afterwards he told me he thought I was finished. Blood was pouring out of my wet suit and I was ghost white. My right hand and arm were so badly slashed that the bones lay bare in several places. My chest, back, left shoulder and side were deeply gashed. Great pieces of flesh had been torn aside, exposing the rib cage, lungs, and upper stomach. All my ribs on the left hand side were crushed, and the shoulder blade had a hole through it where a tooth had pierced the bone. My spleen was uncovered save for a membrane over the top, and the main artery of my heart was pulsing, exposed, just along the side of the bite.

They raced the boat right up onto the rocky reef, not much caring if they destroyed the old wooden craft. Luckily, the boat seats folded down into a six-foot bed. I was only semi-conscious when men swarmed around from everywhere and dragged the boat right out of the water. Frank Alexander, who was president of the skin diver's association, had for the first time in fourteen years driven his car down onto the beach, tired as he was of walking up and down from the parking area on the cliff above with provisions for him, his wife and three kids. The sand had packed just right, so the second the boat ground onto the rocks, Frank drove his car onto the reef, bounding over huge potholes, right to the edge near the boat.

As they lifted me out of the boat the entire side of me opened up and loops of my intestines spilled out and hung down. They quickly rolled me up the other way. Malcom Baker, who had studied first aid for his police examinations, tucked my intestines back with his fingers. They propped me up, stuck me in the back of Frank's Falcon and he blasted back over the reef. Bruce Farley took off as soon as the boat hit the beach, running flat out. He asked the first person he saw where the nearest telephone was. The man was a policeman and knew where to go and what to do, and got an ambulance lined up immediately. In the back of Frank's Falcon, Malcom sat beside me and kept saying, "Keep trying, Rodney. Keep fighting. Just think of Kay and the baby. Come on, you've got to keep breathing!"

I could barely draw a breath. My left lung had collapsed

and was in my throat or in the top of my chest. I kept trying to suck air into my right lung as hard as I could, while everything on my left side gurgled and spuddered. Malcom kept repeating: "You've got to keep going."

I was barely cognizant. I could hear but couldn't understand much of what was happening. My only vivid sensation was swaying in the back of the car as we raced down the road at nearly one-hundred miles an hour. Someone put a hand on my chest and when he took it away I managed somehow to indicate it was better if he kept it there. I could not talk— being too busy trying to breath. I was sucking away with all my might and the hand on my chest stopped the wheezing and gurgling on my collapsed lung.

I heard the shouts: "Here's the ambulance! Stick a shirt out the window! Hang a towel out!" The Falcon screeched to a halt.

They transferred me to the ambulance on a stretcher and immediately gave me oxygen, which was probably the real life-saver of the day. My fellow divers were only too pleased to hand me over to the experts. It told in their voices. It was a miracle that I was still conscious. The doctor said that this was a big factor in my survival. Had I lost consciousness I probably would have died in the Falcon.

Police escorted us all the way to the hospital. From Aldinga to Adelaide is about 34 miles, and every stop light along the way was manned by policemen. We worked out later that from the time I was attacked till the time I reached the hospital was less than an hour.

The surgeons at Royal Adelaide Hospital were scrubbed and ready, the operating table felt warm and cozy, the huge silver light overhead grew dimmer . . . until late that night or early next morning I opened my eyes and saw Kay alongside my bed.

I said, "It hurts," and she was crying. The doctor walked over and said, "He'll make it now."

Today (1964), a year and a half later, my lungs work well, although my chest is still stiff. My right hand isn't a pretty sight, but I can use it. My chest, back, abdomen, and shoulder are badly scarred.

God knows I didn't want to, but Kay realized from the start that I had to go skin diving again. A man's only half a man if fear ties him up. Five months after I recovered, I returned to the sea to leave my fears where I had found them.

The jaws of the great white shark, fringed with a palisade of three-inch scythe-sharp and diamond-hard triangular teeth, are the ultimate in animal weaponry. Jaw muscles will punch the ivory, gleaming points through metal, bone, and cartilage; in a feeding frenzy the great white will take one-hundred-pound bites from his brother's corpus. Poised in front of a two-ton projectile, so beautifully shaped as to yield the very prototype of stealth, so powerfully driven that it can demolish the fabric of a small vessel, the mouth of the great white shark is an established symbol of human horror. Trying to imagine being clutched in the jaws of a great white can only stimulate nightmares.

The last sentence in this story may be the most important; Rodney Fox "returned to the sea to leave my fears where I had found them." Here, in short form, is the timeless, universal antidote to redress any personal trauma: working back through it directly and experientially. And this is exactly the process Fox began when, four months after being torn by the "Great White Death," he donned fins and snorkel and stroked back into the deep.

Fortunately, few of us will ever suffer the depth of trauma that Rodney Fox experienced; but we each carry around some manner of trauma. Fox's courage to return to the scene of his epic and face his fears inspires all of us who feel a periodic chill rattling through our bodies and are too frightened or disconnected to return to the root of our personal wounds. Only when we take Fox's lead and head into our dark waters do we discover, very slowly, that we are more than the demons that prowl there.

J.L.

Credits

"Lion Attack!" is reprinted from *Death in the Long Grass* by Peter Hathaway Capstick (1977) by the permission of St. Martin's Press, New York.

"Rage on the River Zambezi" is reprinted from *Reader's Digest* (February 1997) by the permission of The Reader's Digest Assn. Inc.

"The Muktesar Man-Eater" is reprinted from *The Temple Tiger* by Jim Corbett (1954) by the permission of Oxford University Press, Oxford.

"Assassino" is adapted from *Death in Silent Places* by Peter Hathaway Capstick. Reprinted by the permission of St. Martin's Press, New York.

"Come Quick! I'm Being Eaten by a Bear" is reprinted from *Killer Bears* by Mike Cramond (1981) by the permission Cynthia Dusel-Bacon.

"I Hoped It Would Finish Me Quickly" is reprinted from *Crocodile Attack* by Hugh Edwards (1989) by the permission of HarperCollins Publishers, Inc., New York.

"The Spotted Devil of Gummalapur" by Kenneth Douglas Stuart Anderson (1954) is reprinted by the permission of HarperCollins Publishers, London.

"The Deadly Leopard" is reprinted from *Death in the Dark Continent* by Peter Hathaway Capstick (1983) by the permission of St. Martin's Press, New York.

"Savaged by a Lion" is adapted from *Frozen Terror* by Ben East (1979) by the permission of Crestwood House, Mankato, Minn.

"Night Attack" is reprinted from *Bear Attacks: Their Causes and Avoidance* by Stephen Herrero (1985) by the permission of The Lyons Press, New York.